D1256646

THE DEFENDERS

Also by Geoffrey Cousins:
The Story of Scapa Flow

THE DEFENDERS

A HISTORY OF THE BRITISH VOLUNTEER

by

GEOFFREY COUSINS

with a Foreword by Colonel Sir Tufton Beamish, M.C., M.P.

FREDERICK MULLER
LONDON

First published in Great Britain 1968
by Frederick Muller Ltd., Fleet Street, London, E.C.4.

Copyright © 1968, Cousins Books Limited

Printed in Great Britain
by Ebenezer Baylis and Son, Ltd.
The Trinity Press, Worcester, and London
and bound by Leighton-Straker Bookbinding Co.

To all those who, over many centuries and in countless emergencies, answered the call . . .

"There is no fortification like brave men armed and ready to meet an enemy . . . and such fortification you will always find in the hearts and minds of Englishmen."

LORD PALMERSTON

ILLUSTRATIONS

7

ILLUSTRATIONS

FOREWORD

by Colonel Sir Tufton Beamish, M.C., M.P.

Geoffrey Cousins has chosen an apt moment to trace the history of Britain's volunteer servicemen through nearly 2,000 years to the present day. How inexorably the pattern is repeated: airy unpreparedness, the looming crisis, the call to arms, the violent struggle, the costly victory, always followed by a sanguine determination to get peace on the cheap. Now that we hear the usual contradictory predictions about the nature of future wars and the role of the Armed Forces, this time in a nuclear age, it is important to see the latest re-casting of our volunteer reserves in historical perspective.

The part-time serviceman, so well described by Field Marshal Lord Slim as "twice a citizen", is used to fickle treatment. In times of national danger he will be "handsomely cloathed, most completely Accoutred, mounted on noble Hunters, and treated with Kindness and Generosity" like the eighteenth-century Sussex Light Dragoon on the recruiting poster. In peacetime he may expect political hostility and official indifference. For him as for the professional soldier it is as Kipling said,

> It's Tommy this, an' Tommy that, an'
> 'Chuck him out, the brute!'
> But it's 'Saviour of 'is country' when
> the guns begin to shoot.

Volunteers have borne this constant buffeting without ever losing heart, and the stubborn resistance today to the drastic cuts in the Reserve Forces reflects the same enthusiasm that has survived so many ups and downs.

The Services have always been a melting-pot where professional and amateur, rich and poor find common cause. All fighting men endure the same hardships, honour the same traditions and even enjoy the same jokes, and a competitive spirit between regiments, or between professionals and amateurs, only serves to salt a good relationship. Geoffrey Cousins and I, both Fusiliers, learned this at first-hand during the last War from our respective experiences as part-timer and regular.

The tenacity and ingenuity of the British are often underestimated. They were demonstrated by the Volunteers and Yeomanry who flocked to fight the Boer, and by the Ancient Britons who ferociously resisted invasion. The same strenuous belief in the liberty of the subject fired the God-fearing Cromwellians as it did the clerks and apprentices of London who fought with Simon de Montfort against Henry III at Lewes. Arms and equipment have varied from mace to pick helve, from sling-shot to self-loading rifle, from horse and lance to Chieftain tank and 120 mm. gun. The Defenders have generally fought with courage whatever the weapon or the cause.

Few naval regulars thought that amateur sailors would one day man ships and exemplify the highest naval traditions. Who thought in the 'thirties that the week-end airman would play a crucial part in the Battle of Britain or that women would serve in anti-aircraft batteries? In 1936 many would have agreed with a German view that the Territorial Army was "a sort of Sunday School for amateur soldiers". A few years later those amateur sailors and soldiers, week-end airmen and women in uniform were fighting for this country's survival, and winning.

Like the author I would not care to speculate whether the world will ever again be convulsed by major war, or about the role of the amateur serviceman in a nuclear age. The complexity and destructive power of modern weapons have changed the scale of war, but we surely delude ourselves if we believe the world is at last safer for heroes to live in. Wars apart, man remains subject to flood and fire, earthquake and disease, riot and rebellion, and the spirit of service in which volunteers undertake training and discipline to meet emergencies is an asset we must not squander.

I am very grateful to Geoffrey Cousins for allowing me to add my tribute to the volunteer of every age, whose primary purpose must always be as Lord Haldane said, to put the country "in a state of such security that no one would rashly dare to meddle with us".

TUFTON BEAMISH

INTRODUCTION

THE reorganisation of the Territorial Army in 1967 and complete integration with the Regular Forces of the Crown marked the end of an era which had lasted for the greater part of our recorded history. Although the circumstances varied from century to century and even from dynasty to dynasty, Britons have always been democrats at heart, with a love of freedom and an urge to serve ever among their most striking characteristics. During the negotiations and discussions which led to the reconstruction now completed I was tempted to make some research into the long history of volunteer efforts in these islands, and became the more absorbed the farther I went back into the past. When we recall the stirring of patriotic fervour kindled by threats to home, country and freedom we are recalling events which will probably never be repeated. Perhaps a dangerous statement, having regard to the repetitive habit of history. But it is pertinent, if pessimistic to suggest that if there is to be another world war, a war which might well mean the end of the world, it will begin suddenly without warning, and in a few minutes whole cities might vanish and the surviving inhabitants find themselves involved completely in a struggle of annihilation. For that reason we are unlikely to experience again the spontaneous expression of loyalty and enthusiasm for a cause which marked the rally of citizens to the defence of the nation in 1803, the rush to volunteer for South Africa in 1900, the answer to the call to arms in 1914, and the will to serve which marked the early days of the Second World War.

That may be too sombre a picture of the future. It may be that nuclear warfare will expose some new facet of patriotism, and that individuals outside the Regular Forces (which now include the Territorials) will find opportunities to express their loyalty in times of danger. What is certain is that the past has shown clearly the readiness of the average British citizen to do his duty when faced by an emergency, and his willingness to do whatever he can to make himself ready for taking his place. Through the centuries the part-time soldier has always been with us, and this book is about part-timers who were ready when called upon to be full-timers "for the duration". Britain could never have become a great power and maintained that status for so long without the part-time fighter. She never had a large permanent army (for centuries there was no standing army of any kind) but was usually secure enough at home to be able to throw the greater part of her regular forces, when required, into activities abroad. Britain's overseas commitments have shrunk considerably from those of Victorian and Edwardian days. The advent of long-range missiles, nuclear fission and supersonic flight have made it unnecessary to maintain large conventional forces. But there may still come a chance to test the voluntary spirit, and if history is any guide that need will produce the men. Since the last war we have found new and terrible means of destruction, carried the exploration of space to incredible lengths, and gone a long way along the road to automation and the extinction of the individual. Yet in military matters Britain retains considerable freedom of action. There is still no conscription in Britain in peacetime. The recruiting offices of the Services still get their men and women by invitation, not coercion. And if the reorganisation of the Territorial Army means the virtual end of peacetime volunteering as it was, it also provides the reason for this book.

In approaching the task of setting down in chronological order the development of part-time soldiering in Britain I took the view that too narrow an interpretation of "volunteer" should be avoided. Compulsion has played a comparatively small part in the raising of British forces and even the Derby scheme of 1916 and the conscription laws of the Second World War were designed not only to urge unwilling horses but also to regulate the use of manpower in the best and most economical way. The facts are that when national emergencies arose in 1900, 1914 and 1939 the rush to join up was indicative of a "great heart". That heart has not ceased to beat, even if, in the next emergency, its activities may have to be channelled into many avenues, mostly non-combatant in character.

This then, is a salute to the past accompanied by a confident wave to the future. This is the story of part-timers who could always be counted on to do a good full-time job.

My researches have been concerned mainly with soldiers, since volunteering for the other arms, outside service with the regular forces of the Crown, was a comparatively modern development. Nevertheless the growth of naval volunteering culminating in the formation of the R.N.R. and the R.N.V.R. coincided more or less with the permanent volunteer movement of the 1859–1907 period, and this has been dealt with in Chapter 14. In an appropriately later part of the book I have outlined the development of the air services with particular reference to the Royal Air Force Volunteer Reserve and the Auxiliary Air Force. It is only with some diffidence that I have dealt at any length with the Home Guard; for this force, although a military organisation under the control of the War Office and officered by holders of the King's Commission, was only one of several bodies of both sexes constituting the home front in the greatest threat Britain has ever faced. When so much work was done in dangerous circumstances by the Civil Defence, the National Fire Service, the Ambulance Service, the Women's Voluntary Service, and other units; when so many defence workers in various categories risked and lost their lives in total warfare, it might be thought invidious to single out one organisation for special mention just because its members wore army uniforms. Nevertheless, since the Home Guard was, at least in the eyes of its members, a fighting force, and because its institution was welcomed so enthusiastically by all classes and ages of men, its members deserve to be included among The Defenders whose history is related in these pages.

It would be impossible to mention individually all the many correspondents who have helped in the preparation of this book by contributing personal reminiscences, suggesting references, and in other ways. I have already acknowledged all their letters, and now declare again my thanks for all the assistance given and interest shown. Naturally the greater part of my research was made at the Ministry of Defence Library (Central and Army) in the Old War Office building in Whitehall, and I am deeply grate-full to the Librarian, Mr. D. W. King, O.B.E., F.L.A., who suggested several lines of inquiry; and to the members of his staff, who helped me on so many occasions to find references. For much valuable information about recruiting in the late 1930's and during the Second World War I am indebted to Major-General A. J. K. Pigott, C.B., C.B.E., Director of Recruiting and Mobilization from 1939 to 1945. My research into the history of the London Scottish was greatly helped by Mr. P. Douglas Niekirk and Mr. J. O. Robson, respectively Librarian and Museum Curator at the regiment's headquarters in Buckingham Gate.

So far as literary references were concerned I found Cecil Sebag-Montifiore's "History of the Volunteer Forces" extremely useful, particularly for its reference to various Acts of Parliament and to the works of earlier authors. Another important source of information was "The Story of Our Volunteers" by G. B. Lancaster-Woodbourne, B.A., published in 1881, which provided Sebag-Montifiore with much of his material. Similarly Walter Richards's "His Majesty's Territorial Army", published in 1910, led me to a study of countless Regimental histories, as well as showing the connection between ancient bodies of volunteers and their modern counterparts.

History is full of names but the names change with the epochs, and it is more important to study what is behind the titles than the titles themselves. Thus the Fyrd of Anglo-Saxon times, the General Levy of the Plantagenets, the Trained Bands of the first Elizabeth, the Militia of the 16th and 17th centuries, and the Yeomen and Volunteers of the 18th and 19th, were all representative of the idea of part-time service. And when, early in the 20th century, the Yeomanry and Volunteers were merged into the Territorial Force, it seemed that finality had been reached. But the Territorial Force, after distinguishing itself in one World

War, became the Territorial Army for the second war. Now it has gone through another metamorphosis, and he would be flying in the face of history who declares it is now in its final form.

I have made only a short reference to the latest change, which took place while this book was in preparation; and it would be unwise, so early in the life of the Territorial Army Volunteer Reserve, to pass judgment on the transformation. Interim judgment may be left to the old members of the Territorial Force and the Territorial Army, who have not been slow to criticise the change, and who may be sympathised with in the loss of so much that they worked so hard to preserve. I am content to have derived pleasure from tracing the history of the amateur soldier for nearly 2,000 years; and confident that, no matter how much and to what purpose politicians and military experts interfere with the character and composition of the armed forces of the nation, they will never be able to quench the spirit that has shown itself on innumerable occasions through all those centuries. That spirit of free-born islanders spoke through the lips of Caractacus and flashed from the eyes of Boadicea to endure to the present day. And it will continue to live in British hearts so long as British freedom exists.

1

FIRST there was the home. Then, with the coming of fire, the hearth. And even before the dawn of intellect there was the instinct to defend both against danger from without. Primitive man in his cave slept with club near at hand, ready to crush the skull of the intruder, man or beast. In the beginning this automatic reaction to danger was strictly personal, since one's nearest neighbour was just as much an enemy as the mountain bear or the invader from afar; and only within the family circle could there be security and trust. But another instinct developed with the increase of intellect—the urge to seek help and give assistance. Primitive man began to see in his neighbour not an enemy but an ally. So the communal spirit was born, destined in due time to produce in succession the tribe, the confederation of tribes, the nation, and finally the union of nations.

During what we are pleased to regard as the civilised centuries the primeval instinct to defend hearth and home has developed into a way of life which has been used in many directions for both good and evil. It has been called into action in time of war, exploited by politicians in time of peace, employed by aggressors in the guise of liberators, used for the highest and lowest motives. This was an inevitable consequence of the institution of law and order. With the construction of the community the need for leadership arose. The existence of a tribe necessitated the introduction of an overlord to direct affairs, dispense justice and organise action in the event of a threat to tribal security. In due course the idea of tribal chieftainship, with absolute power vested in one man, gave place to the theory of government by elected representatives of the people. Sometimes, of course, dictatorial powers were assumed by individuals. Whatever the form of government the call to arms usually came from the rulers and was responded to by the ruled, but the fundamental instinct remained, and there were of course many cases where the rulers themselves have been upset by popular desire expressed in popular uprisings. There is no real difference between the savage springing automatically to the defence of his cave and family and the volunteer of modern times enlisting for the protection of the realm or for the overthrow of a tyrant. The trained bands against the Armada, the volunteers raised in fear of a Napoleonic invasion, their successors of Victorian times, the young patriot who fought over the South African veldt, Haldane's Territorials, Kitchener's new army, the bearded grand-dads of the World War I volunteers who guarded the reservoirs and the power stations, the Home Guard of World War II, the fire guards, the Civil Defence workers, the owners of the little boats at Dunkirk, were all actuated by the will to defend what was theirs by all the means in their power. They differed from their primitive ancestors only in the fact that, having been taught respect for authority and being accustomed to regulation, their instincts had to wait on direction.

The cave dweller did not wait for someone to call him to action. That would have had fatal consequences for himself and his dependants. But it would have been equally impossible for the volunteer of modern times to take individual action without consultation with his fellows or instructions from his governors. So, in historical times, the danger has inspired the appeal, and the appeal has led to action.

Inevitably, with the passage of time, and the change of emphasis, the fundamental instinct has been blurred by more sophisticated considerations. When the Romans first came to Britain every man from adolescent to greybeard within range of their threat flew to arms. When Boadicea, scourged and humiliated, rose with the Iceni at her back to avenge her wrongs, she had loyal support not only from her own tribe but also from neighbouring communities. In fact, the whole of East Anglia was

spurred to action. The revolt, involving as it did the sacking of
three of the chief Roman towns, including London, and considerable losses to the legions, was a successful example of how a
people enraged by persecution, oppression and tyranny will rise
spontaneously to defend their territory and their rights. Throughout the history of these islands there have been successive instances
of similar actions, inspired by crises, with the object of defending
country, rights, principles, loved ones, institutions, policies—and
sovereigns.

For this we must thank the tradition of freedom which has
flourished more vigorously and continuously on British soil than
in any other European land. It is the spirit which for centuries
kept us free from a standing army, or suffered one to exist only in
times of emergency and under the control of an elected and
responsible government. This mistrust of royalty and royalty's
favourites meant that in time of war the defence of the realm and
the swelling of the Crown's expeditionary forces depended upon
the efforts of subjects who were fighting men only for the emergency. It was the acquiescence of the yeomen, the freemen, the
squires and the nobles of England over many centuries which
enabled Alfred to fight the Danes, and the kings of England after
the Conquest to wage their wars abroad. Whenever the Normans, the Plantagenets, and the kings of York and Lancaster
crossed the narrow seas to fight the traditional enemies all the
limelight was on the panoply and pomp and excitement of
embarkation. But in the villages and townships the citizens had
been mustered, the communal arms distributed, and every man
who could be spared had gone to his post. And these men were
then, as now, a cross-section of the community. The merchant in
the market place, the blacksmith at his forge, the cowherd in his
byre, the ploughman at his furrow, the yeoman in his hall and
the squire in his manor. These were the men who could and often
did rally to the defence of the homeland; and what the Iceni did
in A.D. 61 was done by bank clerks, labourers, stockbrokers and
shopkeepers in A.D. 1914. The difference was one only of degree.
The character of the driving force had not changed.

There were many changes, of course, in other directions, most of them brought about by the spread of industry and commerce, and the impact on national economy of international affairs. When the call to arms came to primitive man he dropped whatever he was doing and rushed with his weapon to the scene of action. For the period of the emergency the land went untilled and the flocks untended except by the women and children. But this kind of universal rush to repel attack would have been impossible in modern times with the turning of a furrow or the revolving of a power lathe being equally important to any war effort. So eagerness to stand in the breach has now to be subjugated to the overall and varied needs of a nation at war. Even when Britain at last instituted a standing army outside the control of the Crown it was small by Continental standards. A regular military force of a size common in countries with long land frontiers would have been unsuitable to our situation as an island kingdom possessing a large fleet and depending on that for protecting the nation from invasion and maintaining essential supplies. It would certainly have been too grievous a burden on the economy. The feeling of the nation was also against conscription. For these reasons the regular army has always been comparatively small and used in an active sense mainly for expeditions abroad. The safety of the realm, the maintenance of good public order, have mostly been the concern of part-time soldiers, at least until the comparatively modern institution of police forces.

For many centuries home defence was the only duty of these part-time soldiers, whether called levies, militia or volunteers. And even in mid-Victorian days the Volunteers of various kinds were recruited on the understanding that their services were confined to the British Isles. Then came the South African war, and many volunteer battalions not only went overseas, but did "yeoman" service against the Boers. This war forgotten, one of the stipulations concerning the new Territorial Force instituted in 1907 was that no man signed to do more than fight in defence of his country on his native soil. But again, the emergency of 1914 threw these considerations to the wind, and Territorial battalions were specially recruited for Imperial Service. The volunteers of the 1790s and those of the 1900s had at least one thing in common

—they trained in their spare time, served unpaid, were ever ready
to be full-time soldiers in times of crisis, and content to resume
their spare-time role when the emergency ended.

At the end of the 18th century and the beginning of the 19th
there were fears of a Napoleonic invasion of British shores, which
the supremacy of our Navy eventually made impossible. In 1914
the fear of the German hosts was very real and it became necessary, as it might have been in 1794 or 1803, to call on the full
available strength of the nation's manhood. The phrase "available
strength" is used deliberately, for home defence was a much more
complicated business in the 19th century than in the 9th. In both
cases a small proportion of the population was permanently under
arms, and a greater proportion taking arms only for the duration
of the emergency. But taking to arms before the Norman Conquest was a simple matter. The spear, the buckler and the sword
were always ready to hand and every fit man was accustomed
from boyhood to their use. There were no complex problems
about commissariat and supply. The short range of weapons
limited actions in the field to hand-to-hand confrontation of the
rival hosts, and battles therefore were usually of short duration
and almost invariably decided a campaign.

A thousand years later the situation was very different. Arms
had become more complex, more destructive, and naturally more
expensive. Whereas a call by King Alfred for every able-bodied
man who could bear arms would have embraced perhaps eighty
per cent of the adult male population, a similar call by George IV
or William IV would have been responded to by not much more
than ten per cent. And many even in that small category would
have been familiar only with the fencing sword and the pistol—
probably expert with neither and certainly quite ignorant of such
weapons as the musket, the field artillery or the cavalry sabre, to
say nothing of their tactical use in modern warfare. The basic
difference between the situation of Alfred preparing to combat
a Danish attack and the government of George III anticipating a
Napoleonic invasion was that a call to arms among Anglo-Saxons
would have produced a ready-made army requiring only generalship; and any call to the civilian population at the turn of the

18th century would have been useless without a system for training volunteers in the use of arms, and a means of producing the weapons required. The muscles of the populace which constituted the driving force of the Anglo-Saxon armies would not have been sufficient for the Hanoverian generals. They also required the sinews of war—money, armaments, commissariat.

One other difference between the military situation of the Anglo-Saxons and that of the Hanoverian dynasty must be underlined, because it was to become more complex as the life of the country became more mechanised and the economy more prosperous. In the days of Alfred there was very little organised commerce and virtually no organised industry. Local products were mainly food and other perishable items which were in the main consumed locally. Local manufactures might have had a wider circulation, but even this trade would have been conducted by individuals and chiefly by barter. Apart from the gathering of the royal revenues there was no monetary system which employed manpower. But by the time of Napoleon England had a thriving trade system which was world-wide in its scope. We were on the threshold of the industrial revolution at home, in the van of commercial exploitation abroad; and with these developments, as a matter of course, we had a large and complex financial system and an expanding civil service. England had indeed become "a nation of shopkeepers", and many of the "shops" were far from being one-man businesses.

The peasant, yeoman or artisan of Alfred's day could leave his plough, his barn, or his workshop for a few weeks to fight the Danes without upsetting the national life or economy; but any large-scale recruitment of fighting men from among the civil population of Wellington's time would have disrupted the country's industrial and commercial machine. Apart from the fact that by the end of the 18th century the adult male population had for long been accustomed to leaving fighting to those who liked the task and were paid for doing it, the minority who were prepared to rally to the call of danger had to temper their martial ardour by the cold water of civilian requirements. The volunteer system as it developed in those times solved a problem which had become acute. Instead of rushing to the Colours at the call to action, and so endangering the economy of the country and their own individual careers, patriots could learn the art of war in their spare time and so prepare themselves for the hour of their country's need. Even so, those who did volunteer under the Napoleonic threat gave up a great deal to do so. The parsimony of Government, even in the hour of peril, meant considerable personal expense in the majority of cases, relieved in some instances by the generosity of enthusiastic local gentry, or perhaps single rich patrons, who often furnished volunteer units at their own expense.

During the first millenium of the Christian era there was no instance of the inhabitants of England, whether immigrant or indigenous, fighting outside the British Isles, except as individual mercenaries in foreign pay. For 700 years after the Norman conquest our military activity was fairly evenly divided between expeditions abroad and domestic strife or rebellion at home. During the past 300 years, apart from one shortlived and entirely unproductive descent on these shores; the occasional use of soldiery to put down revolts or riots; and, in very recent times, the use of artillery and aircraft against enemy planes, British armed forces have been actively engaged only overseas. It is against this changing pattern that one must plot the development of the Volunteer forces over the 2,000 years of our history as a nation. The march of civilisation changed many things, not least the attitude of man towards his responsibilities as a citizen. And yet we must not be critical of these changed attitudes, nor think that the man "who stayed at home" was necessarily lacking in physical courage. Nowadays there are jobs to be done at home as well as at the front, and in the last fifty years we have had wonderful examples of how a nation threatened by extinction could go to war at home and abroad—men, women, even children—and save their country by their united efforts and their indomitable courage. Nearly two thousand years separated the burning of Londinium by Boadicea and the burning of London by Goering. The centuries between have seen many changes, many shifts of emphasis, many different conceptions of loyalty and service. But the great heart of a nation has beaten steadily through all the years of destructive conflict and constructive peace—and still beats steadily today—the heart of a nation which can give cheerfully and uncomplainingly when danger threatens. The heart of a nation inspired by the true volunteer spirit.

2

ANY survey of these islands, whether from an aeroplane, from a crest of the Sussex Downs, from a church tower in the Fenland, from an escarpment of the Cotswolds, from an eyrie in the Highlands or even by study of photographs, will contribute to a pleasant picture of fields, lakes, streams and woods and moors; scarred, it is true, by the evidence of mechanical industry, but generally giving a sense of prosperity and indicating a sensible and comprehensive use of land. If an aerial picture of Britain 3,000 years ago were available it would show a land of forests, marches and bogs, mainly unproductive, in which the indigenous tribes had carved out small clearings for their own sustenance. A land dark in texture and dark in knowledge, with potential wealth waiting for someone to unlock the door. The first turn of the key was made by the Belgae tribes from Gaul who crossed the Narrow Seas (considerably narrower even than today). They were in search of living room—a compulsive feature of human affairs which has been responsible for most colonisation and for many wars. The pattern set by the Belgae was repeated several times in the next ten centuries, by the Romans, the Saxons and the Norsemen in turn—first exploratory raids, then powerful thrusts seeking permanent footholds, then wholehearted immigration of families, and finally colonisation of the new territory. And the pattern of resistance was also constant. First the desperate resistance of the man in possession threatened by the intruder. Then the gradual submission to superior forces and sometimes higher intellect, and finally integration with the invaders and consequent development of a new composite race.

The general conception of the British of the 1st century B.C. as woad-covered savages living in the woods and sharing acorns with their swine is derived from Roman sources, and invaders are never kind to the invaded in word or action. There can be no doubt that the British of 2,000 years ago were sufficiently cultured to have a complicated religion, forms of tribal government, and intercourse by trade with the Continent, and a considerable degree of artistic appreciation. The early experiences of Julius Caesar, prior to the real Roman invasion, must have convinced him and his legions that he was dealing with a brave, fearless folk who would not easily be subjugated. Julius's first visit was with eighty ships and, meeting with fierce resistance, he lost a great part of his army and retired across the Channel. He came again, with ten times as many ships, it is said, and on this occasion effected a landing. But although by hard fighting the Romans managed to progress as far as the Thames, they were prevented by primitive defences from fording the river. Eventually Julius Caesar, finding it impossible to maintain his men in a hostile region without adequate supplies from abroad, was forced to return once more to his base. A century passed before Britain became a Roman possession, and the conquest started by Claudius in A.D. 47 was not achieved until after fanatical resistance by the natives, considerable bloodshed on both sides, and long and hard campaigns. It might never have been gained at all if the Britons had been as well-organised as the Romans—but that could not be expected. Many valiant hearts beat, but they beat individually. A concourse of tribes under one leader might have defeated the Romans in A.D. 47 just as, 800 years later, a confederacy of Anglo-Saxons under Alfred inflicted many defeats on the Danes. So although our hearts might warm at the pictures of a defiant Caractacus luring the legions to the Welsh fastnesses, and a tragic Boadicea burning Roman towns, there must be set against these the stark fact that the Romans were better armed, better led, employed more effective tactics, and were invincible whenever they confronted the Britons in a pitched battle. Caractacus was taken captive to Rome. Boadicea, to escape a like fate, killed herself, and a page of history was turned. Yet if we turn back that page for a moment we see, running through the pattern of Roman culture and military might overlying the comparatively immature culture of Ancient Britain, the thread of instinctive defence of the homeland which was to run through the pattern of British history for 2,000 years and still glows undimmed in the fabric of our island story.

Resistance to the Romans was not confined to Caractacus and Boadicea. The searchlight of history shines on them and leaves unrecorded many similar instances of Britons refusing to bow beneath the conqueror's yoke. There were pockets of resistance all over southern Britain, and even when the Romans considered themselves masters of the country, they found fortified camps essential to the task of keeping the native population quiescent. The revolt of the Iceni under Boadicea has rightly taken a prominent place in the story of those days, and perhaps there was every reason why it should have been over-glamorised for so many years. My history book at school had a conventional and highly-coloured account of the revolt, accompanied by an equally conventional picture of Boadicea, standing Amazon-like in her chariot, her flowing robes revealing one breast as, steering two frantic, froth-flecked steeds with one hand, she brandished a spear with the other. There were wicked-looking shining sharp knives sticking out from the chariot wheels. Fearsome and romantic—and, oh! so far removed from the truth. Latterday historians have decided that the tragic queen should be known as Boudicca, and archaeologists have proved that her chariots never had scythes on the wheels. I prefer to retain the euphonius name of Boadicea, but the question of the chariot is beyond doubt. The artist who first conceived a chariot as it might have appeared in a Roman stadium, and added to it death-dealing knives of Eastern origin, produced a romantic and inspiring picture. But we now know that the chariots of the Ancient Britons were little more than light carriages used chiefly for conveying spearmen rapidly from point to point of the battlefield, and so creating diversions. These vehicles were no doubt of great value in intertribal warfare when both sides adopted similar tactics, but they had no more than nuisance value against the tight-packed, disciplined legions, who endured the stings of these wasps until the time arrived for a frontal attack. And with the Romans better armed, better protected and invincible at close quarters, the end of such conflicts was always the same.

If the British had been able to sustain their guerrilla tactics, the Romans might have failed to complete the conquest. Julius Caesar, commenting late in life about his campaigns in Britain, described some of these guerrilla attacks and the trouble the heavily-armoured Romans had in dealing with such foes. It was difficult to foresee when an attack was imminent and from what quarter it would come; and impossible to pursue the attackers when they retreated into the woods and marshes from which they had emerged. This was resistance fighting of a type which has been practised throughout history in all parts of the world right down to the present time. But the Britons failed in the end because guerrilla warfare, to be successful, must have an overall command, a central organisation, and a master plan. When Caractacus went to Wales and drew Suetonius Paulinus and his army after him the way was clear for the revolt of the Iceni, enraged and embittered as they were by the oppression of the Roman taxgatherers and the insults to their queen and her daughters. But they merely took advantage of the absence of the main Roman forces. There is no evidence of collusion between Caractacus and Boadicea. Nevertheless, the opportunity was taken and the Iceni by their revolt created a very serious situation for the Romans in London and East Anglia. But the return of the legions led to a pitched battle with the inevitable result.

It is perhaps our national feeling of sympathy for the underdog which makes these stories so heroic. We react in a similar way to the tales of Alfred the Great, Hereward the Wake and other heroes of resistance movements. But even when shorn of romantic trappings, the actions of the Ancient Britons in defying the invaders can be regarded as clear examples of fighting fervour inspired by the purest of motives—defence of home, hearth and country. The rude warriors who fought under Caractacus and Boadicea were unpaid, part-time, virtually untrained, but also desperate, vengeful and fearless. They were no doubt volunteers from necessity, but the spirit which moved them is the same spirit which moves the volunteer of today—undimmed by the passing of the centuries.

3

DURING the three centuries which followed the defeat of the Iceni the Romans not only controlled most of what is now England but also protected it efficiently against the ancient Celtic tribes who still maintained independence beyond their borders. The conquerors also integrated the indigent population into a way of life which, being luxurious and social, depended for its maintenance on imports from abroad and the presence of a strong, efficient Roman garrison. When this army was withdrawn in A.D. 410 because of the siege of Rome the Britons whose ancestors had fought so heroically against Caesar, Claudius and Severus found themselves unable to stand alone against the Picts, the Scots and the Welsh. This situation was due less to the inability of the populace to fight than to the pusillanimity of their leaders, who had become romanised in their way of life and too long dependent upon the Roman sword. So the principal chief of that time, Vortigern, looked round for another helping hand. For many years trade had been in progress between the Roman-Britons and the Continent, and the existence of warlike tribes in the low lands across the sea was well known. It was to one of these tribes, the Angles, that Vortigern turned for support. They were invited to establish themselves in Britain on condition that they fought against the Picts and Scots. The first Angles came ashore at Ebbsfleet in Kent and were given land there. Needless to say, this action by Vortigern was to lead to the subjugation of his people to another set of rivals. When the Angles saw the fertile lands of Kent and the excellent living conditions of the Romano-British, and realised also that the local leaders were effete, with a preference for negotiation rather than fighting, they seized the opportunity for permanent colonisation. So came not only more Angles but also Jutes and Saxons, with their families. Hengist and Horsa came, and after them Cerdic the Saxon, who was to conquer the whole of Southern England by the beginning of the sixth century. It would be wrong to suggest that all these intrusions met with no material resistance. The Romano-British leaders might be more prone to treat than to fight, but the populace viewed with dismay the inroads of these vigorous, intrepid men from across the sea who, like the Picts and Scots, fought unarmoured with spear and buckler; and they resisted in a way that common people have resisted throughout history.

The invasions of the Saxons (to give a generic name to an assembly of different tribes), was entirely different from the Roman conquest. The Romans came in orderly legions under a supreme command. The Saxons came in small independent companies landing at different points, each company acknowledging its own leader and having no co-ordination with other marauding parties. If the Saxons had been combined into a big force under one overlord and had planned their invasion operation on the lines of the Roman conquest there is no doubt they would rapidly have overrun the country. As it was their sporadic, widely-separated and unco-ordinated raids were resisted to such an extent that conquests were achieved only at great length and at heavy cost.

The appearance of a Saxon ship or fleet off the coast was the signal for an array of defenders to assemble. Often the pirates had to sail away to find a less well-defended spot, and if they did land it was often to be involved in heavy fighting for the tenuous foothold obtained. But if the Saxons of the 5th century suffered from lack of co-ordination so did the Romano-British. They also operated as independent units each concentrating on the immediate local threat and having no guidance or support from a central authority. So the issue depended on fighting ability, and the warlike Saxons prevailed in the end.

The tribal divisions of the Saxons in their early raids on Britain were maintained when they became masters of the country, for it was split up into a number of kingdoms. Those who had operated in Kent and Sussex formed one kingdom. Those who had landed in East Anglia formed the Kingdom of that name. Those who had invaded further North became the Mercians and the Northumbrians, and those who had pushed to the West founded the Kingdom of Wessex. Obviously the existence of separate kingdoms meant internecine warfare which lasted until the whole nation became one under the technical overlordship of Egbert in the 9th century.

The establishment of a complete Saxon kingdom in Britain had many sequels of importance, not least the beginning of a regular military system which, despite many changes in detail over the centuries, has persisted in its fundamentals to the present day. The Saxon king was not only the political ruler of his people but also their leader in battle. His chief men, the *gesiths*, were not only advisers to him in council but also his generals in the field. And the freemen (*ceorls*), although primarily concerned with the cultivation of land and the affairs of their immediate localities, were available to fight under the King's command when required to do so.

The *gesith* was bound by oath to the king and could be heavily penalised, by loss of land and money, if he failed to give the military service demanded of him. There were also penalties for *ceorls* who failed to toe the line when the forces of the kingdom were mustered. But these men were not professional soldiers. They were the forerunner of the militia, who led normal lives until an emergency arose, and were not "paid soldiers" except for what subsistence they received while actually engaged in fighting.

The national force so described was known as the "fyrd", but until the days of King Alfred it was an ill-organised ill-armed body, and the battles between the various Saxon kingdoms were decided mainly by the rival *gesiths* or *thegns*, surrounding and supporting their respective leaders. This was the situation when, towards the end of the 8th century, a new menace from overseas became evident. This time the threat was not against the South-East coast but along the North-East coast; and the marauders were the terrible North-men from Scandinavia. In 793 the Norsemen made a plundering raid on the Northumbrian coast and among other acts of rapine destroyed the church on Lindisfarne island. This was but the beginning, and during the next seventy years the Danes grew ever more powerful, penetrating deeply into the country. From isolated raids on Northumberland they proceeded to big attacks on all parts of the English coast from Durham to Cornwall, and by the middle of the 9th century had begun to winter in England, thus establishing strong colonies. The pattern of the Saxon invasions was in fact being repeated, the Saxons this time being on the receiving end. And as they in the past had fought and treated as it suited their policies, so the Danes used the sword and the conference table according to circumstances and with equal ruthlessness and cynicism. Here again we had a repetition of the internal situation of previous races. The British could not prevail against the Romans because the enemy were better armed, better drilled and formed a cohesive force under one commander. The Romano-British were beaten and absorbed by the Saxons because they lacked cohesion and had no central direction. Now the Saxons were losing to the Danes for the same reason. The situation demanded a consolidation of the defending forces under a resolute, fearless and sagacious leader and this was to come about. The rise of Egbert, described with doubtful justification as the first king of all England, led to alliances of the Saxon kingdoms. In 851 occurred one of the biggest Danish onslaughts. They came with 350 ships up the Thames, sacked London, put the Mercians to flight, and then met the West Saxons under Aethelwulf and were beaten decisively. So they left the West Saxons severely alone and concentrated on weaker points. One of these was Mercia, and Burgoed, king of the Mercians, appealed for help to Ethelred, then King of Wessex, and his brother Alfred. The West Saxons and the Mercians joined forces and were on the point of gaining a decisive victory over the Danes when the invaders put away the sword and offered the olive branch, with inevitable results. But it was now clear that the military ardour of the West Saxons, with Alfred claiming the kingship of all England, could be a decisive factor in the battle

ALL thofe who prefer the Glory of bearing Arms to any fervile mean Employ, and have Spirit to ftand forth in **Defence** of their **King** and **Country**, againft the treacherous Defigns of *France* and *Spain*, in the

Suffex Light Dragoons,

Commanded by

Lt. Col. John Baker Holroyd,

Let them repair to

Where they fhall be handfomely Cloathed, moft compleatly Accoutred, mounted on noble Hunters, and treated with Kindnefs and Generofity.

An eighteenth-century recruiting poster for the Sussex Light Dragoons

Meeting of the Inhabitants

OF THE PARISHES OF

Worlingworth, Southolt, Athlington, Horham, Wilby, Brundish, Saxtead, Bedfield, and Tannington,

HELD IN THE PARISH OF WORLINGWORTH,

On *Tuesday*, the 15th Day of *May*, 1798.

JOHN HENNIKER MAJOR, Efq. in the Chair.

RESOLVED UNANIMOUSLY, That we hold ourfelves bound in Duty and Gratitude at all Times to affift in endeavouring to fupport and maintain the Happy Conftitution of this Country, and to contribute every Affiftance in our Power, collectively and individually, to the due Execution of the Laws, the Maintenance of Civil Order and Good Government, and the immediate Suppreffion of all Riots and Tumults, under what Pretence foever they may be excited, or for what Caufe foever they may arife.

Refolved unanimoufly, That a Corps of Infantry be formed by the Name of the LOYAL WORLINGWORTH VOLUNTEERS, to be raifed, exercifed, and employed in any Place within the Parifhes abovementioned; Government finding Arms and Accoutrements, with fuch Proportion of Ammunition as may be neceffary for the Ufe of the Corps; Government alfo finding a Drill Serjeant, a Drummer and a Fifer.

Refolved unanimoufly, That they fhall not be called out except in Cafe of Actual Invafion or eminent Danger thereof, as explained in an Act of Parliament lately paffed, or in Cafe of Riot or Tumult, and in no cafe to be called out to do Duty beyond the Bounds of the faid Parifhes.

Refolved unanimoufly, That they fhall not be drafted or added to any other Corps.

Refolved unanimoufly, That Government be requefted to find Arms, Accoutrements, and Ammunition, and that the Corps do find the Drefs at the Appointment of the Officers.

Refolved unanimoufly, That the Officers at prefent confift of a Captain and two Lieutenants, and that they be recommended to the Lord Lieutenant by the Corps.

Refolved unanimoufly, That JOHN HENNIKER MAJOR, Efq. be requefted to accept the Commiffion of Captain, and that he be recommended accordingly to the Lord Lieutenant for that Purpofe.

Refolved unanimoufly, That the Rev. CHARLES BUCKLE be requefted to accept the Office of Treafurer to this Affociation.

Refolved unanimoufly, That Mr. SAMUEL RAY be recommended as Firft Lieutenant, and Mr. William Ray, as our Second Lieutenant.

Refolved unanimoufly, That every one of the above-mentioned Parifhes, joining the Parifh of Worlingworth in this Affociation, appoint one Committee Man, and that the Parifh of Worlingworth appoint feven Perfons for the faid Committee.

Refolved unanimoufly, That three or more of the Perfons above fpecified be a Committee, one of the Officers, the Captain, or either of the Lieutenants of the faid Volunteer Corps, or the Treafurer of the fame being prefent.

Refolved unanimoufly, That the Corps be regularly trained and exercifed in fuch Manner and at fuch Times as fhall be appointed by the Committee.

Refolved unanimoufly, That a Subfcription be opened for carrying into Effect the above-mentioned Refolutions, and that the Money arifing therefrom be lodged in the Hands of the Treafurer, and be under the Care and Management of the faid Committee

Refolved unanimoufly, That the Committee meet for the firft Time at the SWAN INN in the Parifh of Worlingworth, on Thurfday the 24th Inftant, at Six O'Clock in the Afternoon, to receive further Signatures, and to tranfact other Bufinefs relating to the faid Corps.

Refolved unanimofly, That thefe Refolutions be publifhed once in the Bury Paper and once in the Ipfwich Journal, and that the Chairman be requefted to difpatch them without delay to the Lord Lieutenant for the Approbation of his Majefty.

JOHN HENNIKER MAJOR, Chairman.

Refolved unanimoufly, That the Thanks of this Meeting be given to the Chairman, for his great Attention to the Bufinefs of the Meeting, and his Conduct in the Chair.

Refolved unanimoufly, That the Thanks of this Meeting be given to the Treafurer, for the Active and Obliging Intereft he has taken in the Formation of this Corps.

JOHN FISHER,

Clerk to the above Affociation.

Notice of a meeting held in 1798 in the parish of Worlingworth, Suffolk, to form an armed body of volunteers against the Danes. The death of his brother, Ethelred, left Alfred to begin a career of quarter of a century which was to leave its mark on history. It may be open to argument whether Alfred the Great was really the father of the British Navy, but there is no doubt whatever that he was responsible for the foundation of our military system. The vacillations of the kings who followed Alfred led eventually to the subjugation of the English first by the Danes and then by the Normans. But Alfred's institutions remained as monuments to his wisdom and greatness. One of these was the intelligent use of the fighting forces of the realm. Until his day a call to arms had been answered by everyone available. But Alfred realised that the maintenance of agriculture, manufacture and trade was just as important as the waging of successful war. So he had two armies instead of one. While half the men available for service were in the field the other half were in the fields. By these means Alfred had ready to hand an instrument of war and at the same time ensured not only that the essential services of the home front were carried out, but also that the villages, towns and settlements were not entirely unprotected against diversionary raids by the enemy.

The value of this division of the "fyrd" into two parts was seen in 893 when the Danes, by now firmly established in Kent, harried the inhabitants of the fertile lands of the Sussex Weald, making onslaughts from the wooded Downs to the North and the South. They met with resistance and eventually gathered what booty they could get and made off towards their strongholds. Then King Alfred's main army fell on them, put them to flight and recovered the booty.

But the reign of Alfred passed, and that of the equally warlike Athelstan and Edmund, his successors to the kingdom of Wessex, and the remainder of the 10th century saw the gradual subjugation of the Anglo-Saxons to the Danes as a result of indecision, unpreparedness, cowardice and pacification, not unmixed with treachery and double-dealing. The desperate courage of the ordinary inhabitants, springing from the richest moral sources, was insufficient while their rulers were buying uneasy peace and relying on the flimsy promises of cynical and ruthless enemies.

In 1001 Ethelred made peace with the Danes at a cost of £24,000 but this was merely deferring the inevitable end. Sweyn and his brother Olaf with their followers were in virtual control of the whole country by 1009 and five years later Sweyn's son Canute became the first undisputed Danish king of England. The Saxon line was restored twenty-five years later, but only to put on the throne a peaceable, monkish monarch who made the same mistakes as his predecessors, who had chosen to negotiate rather than defy. When the brief reign of Harold came to its tragic end England fell like a ripe plum into the cultured, sophisticated hands of the Normans. The age of chivalry had begun, and with it a whole new conception of war and the character of those who waged it.

Prior to the establishment of the brief Danish dynasty in England any assembly of armed men was brought into existence only for the purposes of war and remained under arms only for the duration of the emergency. When every able-bodied male was accustomed to fighting and weapons of some kind were always at hand, there was need only for the call. Sometimes even the call was superfluous—the imminent danger itself being the spur to action. The Anglo-Saxon court, too, consisted merely of the King, his family and retainers and advisers, all armed as a matter of course and ready to take their places in the battle array when required. But the idea of regular household troops always in commission began with the accession of Canute. The son of Sweyn had consolidated his father's brief authority by the importation of a big army from Denmark, and when the country was quiet he sent home only part of this force. Some thousands were kept in England as a royal bodyguard known as *huscarles*. The strength of this force suggested that although perhaps nominally a bodyguard charged with the protection of King and court, it was in fact a permanent nucleus around which the King could build a large army in time of need. Certainly it can be regarded as the first example of a standing army. Once in being the huscarles persisted in one form or another, and came to be regarded not only as troops regularly employed in and around the royal household but also as the elite of the army in battle. At Hastings Harold put his huscarles in the centre of his army, and William won that battle because he concentrated on the Anglo-Saxon wings, where cohesion was lacking and discipline weakest.

The Norman Conquest, of course, brought in its train many social and political changes in the government of England, including an entirely new conception of military service. To understand fully the impact of this change we must consider further the development of the fyrd, which, until the Conquest, formed the bulk of the armed forces of the land, despite its part-time character. In the early days of the Anglo-Saxon era the family was more important than the State, and local feuds aroused greater passions than the quarrels of nobles or kings. But once the primitive idea of an eye for an eye and a tooth for a tooth gave place to the legal requirements of the *wergild* for causing death, the thoughts of men were turned to events and considerations outside those of the immediate family. The *wergild* itself, by recognising distinctions among men (for it cost more to slay a nobleman than to kill a churl) paved the way towards military distinctions on which all subsequent military policies have been based.

The fyrd was in effect a people's army. Three services were required of it—the building of fortifications, the repair of bridges, and military service in defence of the kingdom. Every freeman and every landowner between 16 and 60 was obliged to do fyrd duty under pain of severe penalties, including loss of land. In 866 Ethelred had ordained: "If anyone without leave return from the fyrd (in which the King himself is) let it be at his own peril of himself and his estate".

It seems clear that the assembly of the fyrd in time of need was a fairly haphazard process, and until it was complete and the King in personal command of the array few men knew the actual composition of the force. In time, of course, some kind of organisation developed. The bulk of the force consisted of the freemen (*ceorls* or *churls*) and they were recruited and commanded by the *eorls* (earldormen). Each earldorman was responsible for the forces in his shire, and was therefore the forerunner of the Lord-Lieutenant, who has been responsible in more recent times for the recruitment and control of militia, volunteers and Territorials in succession.

It would be wrong to assume that the fyrd, at least before Alfred's reign, was a well-trained well armed body which could be called into action and immediately used as a cohesive force. Enthusiasm was no doubt there to some degree, but of training there was little or none; and arms, where they existed, were of a rudimentary character. Armour, too, was practically non-existent in "the ranks". This will explain how comparatively small numbers of Scandinavians were able to prevail over the local forces.

The fyrd system as it developed had another drawback which was to be accentuated when, under the Normans, the fyrd gave place to the feudal system. The earldormen, as their power and authority increased with their responsibilities, grew into petty princelings and tended by their own aggrandisement to weaken the authority of the Crown. This tendency was checked to some extent by the "huscarle" system of the Danish kings. By increasing the size and effectiveness of their immediate forces they were able to increase the kingly power and thereby restrict the scope of the earldormen. Yet the seeds had been sown. The power of the provincial chiefs grew again under the Normans, and for centuries there were constant clashes between the monarch and his proud, unruly and self-sufficient barons. Nevertheless, the advantages of the Danish system outweighed the disadvantages. When an emergency arose the king had not to wait for the *thegns* of the counties to assemble. The household troops were always ready to hand as the first bastion of defence or the vanguard of the attack, to be supported eventually by the shire levies. The system worked well enough until the Battle of Hastings proved that an army of mercenaries and adventurers, skilled in arms and fighting strategy and kept in order by a leader who was also a disciplinarian, would always prevail over a fervent but unbalanced national force of the kind with which Harold opposed the Conqueror. The day of the permanent, full-time fighting mercenary had arrived, and not for a long time would the part-time soldier have a really effective part to play in the military affairs of the nation.

4

FOR more than a century after the Conquest the fyrd was relegated to a subsidiary role and in fact passed into history, to be succeeded in later times by the militia. The armed power of the nation under the Normans was represented by the feudal host, contributed to by barons and their retainers who had come over with William the Conqueror, their descendants, and mercenaries from the Continent. Much of the fighting on British soil between kings and rebellious noblemen up to the time of Stephen's campaign against Matilda (1141–45), was carried out by Frenchmen, Germans and Flemings, who depended for sustenance and reward less on the purses of their employers than on the resident population, which suffered much from their extortions. With the accession of Henry II in 1145 came a big change for the better, and from this period we can begin to trace the development of the militia, or what might be called the folk-army as distinct from the feudal host. The catalyst was the Assize of Arms of 1181, described by Fortescue (*The History of the British Army*) as 'the earliest enactment for the organisation of our national forces, and the basis of all that followed down to the reign of Philip and Mary."

The Assize of Arms required all freemen to equip themselves with arms and armour as their means allowed, but had one important provision which was very much in line with the democratic thinking of more modern times. The liability of each man concerned was to be determined not by the arbitrary decisions of local chiefs, but by legal juries appointed to consider every

37

case on its merits. In detail the Assize of Arms declared that:

Every holder of one knight's fee (or fief) should have a coat of mail, a helmet, a shield and a lance, and every knight as many coats of mail, helmets, shields, lances as there were fees in his domain.

Every free layman having in chattels or rent to the value of 16 marks should keep the same equipment.

Every free layman having in chattels or rent 10 marks should keep a habergeon, a chaplet of iron and a lance. (A habergeon was a small coat of mail without sleeves, and a chaplet an iron skull cap without visor).

All burgesses and the whole community of freemen should have each a wambais (a padded doublet covered with leather), a chaplet and a lance.

We can see in these provisions, and those of the Statute of Winchester enacted in 1285 in the reign of Edward I, the beginnings of the idea of local recruitment and control of the forces of the realm, a characteristic which has persisted through the centuries to the present day, when practically every Territorial unit is identified with a county, and many regular regiments have well-defined district or racial associations. The reforms started by Henry II in fact repeated the general idea of the fyrd with important improvements in organisation and administration.

The vital factor in this reform was the spread of responsibility to all sections of the community. Hitherto the barons had been left to their own devices in making their contribution to the feudal host. A proper quota had been required of each nobleman, according to his rank and possessions; but there was no official control over, or even interest in, the methods he adopted to raise the appropriate force. Now, however, while the holder of a knight's fee was still expected to make the largest contribution, the landed freeman of the first class was ranked as of equal importance; and even the lowliest freeman in terms of possessions was expected to play his part. The enactment so wisely made by Henry II laid the foundations of the National Militia, a force which represented the real military strength of the nation until the institution of a regular army in Stuart times. Stubbs in his *Constitutional History of England* takes the view that the re-organisation of the nation's forces on a free national basis was due to a general discontent with the situation caused by the existence of both a feudal array and the fyrd in combination with the practice of importing mercenaries from abroad. The king in these circumstances was in a powerful position. He could use the barons' forces and his militia for warfare abroad and bring mercenaries into England to keep his people under subjection. Henry II's reforms, by ending the use of foreign troops and checking the excesses of the barons, strengthened the power of the freemen; and the freemen, by refusing to serve abroad and concentrating their efforts on the proper organisation of military forces at home, gradually evolved the strongest possible weapon of defence, administered by the people for the people.

This was the dawning of democracy and the influence of the common man. After centuries of subjection to kings and nobles the free citizens of England enthusiastically shouldered the responsibilities of fighting men, knowing they were to fight not on foreign soil for the satisfaction of aggressive ambition, but on their own soil for the protection of the fatherland. Maybe there were many in those days who tried to avoid this responsibility. There were shirkers, no doubt, and deserters, and evaders; even, perhaps, conscientious objectors. But a new spirit had been born —a spirit which was to have permanence in the hearts of British people—the spirit of service for the country.

Of course the foreign mercenary did not immediately disappear from the English landscape. But after the Assize of Arms these professional soldiers were recruited abroad, used in the battles against France, and rarely set foot in England, much to the relief of the inhabitants. Probably the last occasion on which mercenaries fought on any scale in England occurred during the rebellion of the Earl of Leicester, who brought over 3,000 Flemish mercenaries to East Anglia to assist him in his design. For years past foreign paid soldiers had earned the hatred of the whole nation. The freeman who had had his crops destroyed or stolen, his home invaded, and maybe his wife and daughters insulted by foreign soldiers, could not be expected to look with favour on or support the cause of noblemen who had recourse to hiring fighters from abroad. His sympathies and those of his underlings were bound to be with the native forces and their leaders, and the national spirit owed its development not only to patriotism but also to respect for law and order and a sense of self-preservation. Patriotism is an overworked term anyway. "My country right or wrong" is a challenging slogan, but not so powerful as the ancient instinct to defend hearth, home and dependants. The yeoman farmer of the 12th century who went to do battle with his lance or his sword and jerkin, and the yokel who joined in with his stave or pitchfork, were not actuated primarily by the necessity to defend the whole country. They were influenced mainly by local considerations and concerned only with their particular districts. The effectiveness of this local spirit was seen in 1173 when the Earl of Leicester marched with his English supporters and his 3,000 Flemings towards the Midlands. Humphrey de Bohun, Constable of England, gathered what forces he could in the effort to check the advance, but was able to muster only a few hundred knights and their followers. But very quickly the royal army received great reinforcement provided by the shire levies of Suffolk, Cambridgeshire and Norfolk, who, with painful memories of the ravages of other Flemings in East Anglia, were determined to drive these foreigners out of the country. With the assistance of these local forces, inspired by local considerations and full of fighting fervour even if neither so well armed nor so experienced as the Flemings, De Bohun was able to end the rebellion.

No doubt many brave men fell in this conflict because they were inferior in arms and armour. But the battle was won because the freemen of England, or at least of East Anglia, fought in defence of their homes and their rights, and so had a spirit which enabled them to overcome those who had neither a cause nor a worthwhile objective.

Nearly a century later, in the troubled times which led to the formation of the first British parliament, itself a milestone on the road to democratic government, the men of London, marshalled

and led by an Alderman, Thomas of Pevelsdon, marched in the
army of Simon de Montfort and fought at the Battle of Lewes in
1264. Simon de Montfort did not long survive Lewes. He was
killed a year later at the Battle of Evesham. But the great baron,
by his insistence on democratic principles in an age accustomed to
rule by force, had wrought a remarkable change in the attitude of
the Plantagenet kings to the government and protection of the
country. We were to see, unfortunately, more than one relapse
from this high standard of government. The Wars of the Roses
and the Civil War had yet to come. But in the 13th century the
reforming seed sown by Henry II, first of the Plantagenets, had
grown fruit; and the next great move forward came in 1285 with
the Statute of Winchester which among other things obliged
every man to have in his house "harness for to keep the peace",
and every man between 15 and 60 to be "assessed and sworn to
armour", with swords, knives "and other weapons". Forty years
later the rights of the individual had advanced so much that an
Act was passed ordaining "that no man be compelled to go out of
his shire but where necessity requireth," and that no man could
be pressed into military service. The principle that any who
volunteered for the King's service must be paid by the King was
admitted in 1344, and seven years later it was declared "that no
man be constrained to feud of arms except by common assent
and grant made in Parliament."

The principles underlying these measures were not always to be
observed in the turmoils and political changes of the next three
hundred years, but Edward III had certainly brought about an
important and fundamental change in the country's military structure when he introduced a paid army for his foreign wars, by
nominating leading nobles to recruit fighting men under precise
conditions of service. The conditions governed such matters as
pay, rank, tenure of service, and provision of arms. There was
even a clause providing for the indented soldier to "sign on" for
a further period of service. By these means Edward III was able
to build up an army which had many of the characteristics of the
national forces of the 19th and 20th centuries. Instead of having to
rely on the goodwill and loyalty of the barons and big landowners

in recruiting, equipping and leading their retainers, the King could be sure of a professional or semi-professional army; and, by the system of short-service indentures (usually one year) could ensure a constant supply of men who had had some training in the use of arms and the art of war. To some extent these moves of Edward III had been forced on him by circumstances. Even under the reign of Edward I the barons had shown an increasing reluctance to undertake warfare abroad. They had upset Edward I's grandiose schemes for conquering France by their unwillingness to participate in expeditions across the Channel. But when it was a question of defending the home country there was no lack of enthusiasm. The Scots took advantage of the preoccupations with France to attack across the Border, but in the face of this threat the whole military might of England, from feudal bands to shire levies, went into action.

Edward III was wise to distinguish between foreign wars and home defence, and the fighting machine he developed was used to achieve the victories of Crécy and Poitiers. The king had his cavalry, his archers, his men-at-arms, and all ancillary services under their various commanders, responsible to his generals and through them to himself. The knights and noblemen who fought in his army did so for pay, just as did the archers and men-at-arms. And back at home the security of the realm was largely in the keeping of the shire levies and their local commanders. Thus we had at last the distinction, and an important one, between the professional and the non-professional soldiers. It is a distinction which should be emphasised as often as possible, for to take a very narrow interpretation of the term "volunteer" is to do injustice to many brave men down the centuries who have fought and suffered for their country with no more than a nominal reward and with no hope of renown. Some purists would argue that a volunteer is one who acts entirely of his own volition and not under pressure of any kind. But what is pressure? In its highest form it can be an instinctive urge to serve one's country when it is endangered. It could take the form of an appeal to one's patriotism, which is one degree removed from the purely instinctive dash into action. It could be the insistent pressure of a friend, or even the weighty suggestion of an employer. The love of adventure, or a predilection for the company of one's fellow-men, must also be considered as influences which might tend to "volunteering".

It cannot be doubted that of those summoned to the shire levies of Plantagenet times were many who jibbed at the idea of service, even for a short time, and would resort to any possible device to dodge their responsibilities. But there were also many who welcomed the call to arms as an opportunity to exercise a patriotic spirit, or from a love of action and adventure, or a genuine wish to carry arms and use them in earnest when the occasion arose. But whether reluctant or ardent, the part-time soldier of those days was a non-professional, just as the Militia, the Yeomanry, the Volunteers and the Territorials were in their successive periods. And as gifted amateurs in any walk of life can often equal or excel the professional performer, so in military affairs the transition from non-professional to professional can often be so slight as to be unnoticeable. We have the evidence of the South African war and the two world wars to show that a part-time soldier having a reasonable acquaintance with the use of arms and the order of drill can quickly be assimilated into a regular force, without decreasing, and often actually increasing, the efficiency of the unit he joins.

The armies of Edward III differed little in fundamentals from those of William III. The Wars of the Roses disrupted the idea of a unified Royal command, and when the country was finally at peace men's thoughts began to turn away from wasteful foreign wars towards the development of trade and social life under peaceful conditions at home. In this way the amateur soldier began to be much more important than his professional counterpart. Law and order were maintained by the justices and their constables, and when they were unable to control riots or civil disorder the gentry and the yeomen were there to act in their support.

The praise of the yeomen of England has been sung over the years. In Tudor times the yeoman was the real strength of the country. Whether a freeholder of land, a gentleman farmer, a

squire of the manor or a peasant smallholder, the yeoman produced the real wealth of England at that time—its agriculture.
And when he went to war he did so willingly in defence of his
king, his country and his property, returning no less willingly to
his normal occupation when the emergency ended. Much of the
peaceful and pleasant existence of the English people during the
greater part of the Tudor dynasty and the early Stuart reigns was
due to the absence of a standing army, or indeed of any sizable
force under the control of the king. The country had suffered
much from the ravages of the Wars of the Roses, and no longer
was a true, free Englishman going to be subject to the oppression
and tyranny of professional soldiers and their masters. It is true
that the conspicuous failure of English arms abroad in Tudor
times was consistent with the absence of trained regular soldiers.
But aggressive campaigns abroad had gone out of favour, and
with the loss of Calais under Mary we entered a long period of
military peace at home and colonisation abroad. There was,
indeed, a shift of emphasis from military to naval considerations.
As the power of military England declined so her power on the
high seas and in the narrow waters waxed, mainly as a result of the
activities of sea captains and merchant adventurers in searching for
new lands and exploiting the wealth they held. Under Henry VIII
the Navy became a regular force and very quickly developed into
what it has since always been—the bulwark of a maritime island
nation.

It was only the Navy which prevented the invasion of England
by Spanish troops. If the British sailors had not, by superb sea-
manship and great courage—aided by the weather—broken up
the Armada and forced it to flee to destruction, a Spanish landing
could have taken place in which case the yeomen of England
forming the defensive militia might have found themselves
inadequate in arms and training for the task of repelling the well-
armed and armoured veterans of Spain. The situation confronting
England's defenders then might be likened to the situation in
which Britain found herself after Dunkirk, when the Local
Defence Volunteers (afterwards the Home Guard) were recruited
to "fight them on the beaches", etc. There was tremendous

enthusiasm for this idea and thousands of men, including many
veterans of previous wars, jumped at the opportunity to repel
possible invaders. But with the advantage of hindsight we can
realise that such a force, operating in small units up and down the
country, would have found it difficult to prevent the success of an
airborne and seaborne invasion on the scale which the Germans
planned and of a type which we ourselves launched successfully
on the Continent four years later. In our predicament in the
autumn of 1940 it was our command of the air, as well as our
command of the seas which averted the danger. Nevertheless,
the volunteer spirit was there as it had been all down the centuries, and history is also full of examples of how even volunteers,
ill-armed and ill-trained in comparison with the enemy, have
preserved their country and their homes, by the successful waging
of guerrilla warfare.

5

THE latter part of the 16th century saw the modest beginnings of the volunteer movement. There is no intention to give priority of genesis to any individual or unit, but the Cheshire Yeomanry, which dates officially from November, 1796, traces its descent from a band of "Cheshire Yeomen" who fought at the Battle of Blore Heath in 1459. A contemporary account of the battle, quoted in the regimental history, relates how the Cheshire Yeomen were the greatest sufferers among the troops which took part. They all wore the little silver swan, the Prince of Wales's badge, "which the Queen had ordered to be distributed among the gentlemen of that county". This was in the early stages of the Wars of the Roses, and the Queen was Margaret of Anjou. What was true of Cheshire was true no doubt of many other counties in those troublous times, with country squires and farmers riding at their own expense in support of one faction or the other, and perhaps many another county regiment could by these tenuous means trace its descent from the 15th century. In 1469 there was a volunteer operation of a different kind—the rising of Robin of Redesdale inspired by Warwick the Kingmaker in his efforts to rouse the country against Edward IV's alliance with Burgundy. Twenty years later, with the death of Edward and the flaring-up of trouble over the succession, the need for the preservation of law and order in the countryside became paramount, and in 1483 the "fencible"—a man recruited for local defence and protection—made his bow. "Defensible personis", it was ruled, could be all men between 16 and 60 capable of bearing arms, with no distinction of rank or wealth. There can be no doubt that "fencibles" formed a large part of the forces which flocked to the standard of Henry Tudor when he landed at Milford Haven on his way to Bosworth Field and the crown. And yeomen of many a county must have fought and fallen on both sides in that decisive conflict.

With Henry VII firmly established on the throne the way was clear for peace, constructive government and subsequent prosperity. No grandiose schemes for aggression abroad, no fear of further strife at home. Therefore no need for a mercenary army, or indeed any army at all save that which could be summoned in emergency from the manor, the farm, the cottage and the workshop. In these circumstances it might be thought that the King in his palace was perhaps the least protected inhabitant in the island, and this no doubt inspired Henry VII to institute a 16th-century equivalent of the Anglo-Saxon huscarles. Shortly after his succession in 1485 he established a body of "Yeomen of the Guard", a force of some 200–300 gentlemen of good birth volunteering to serve the King in this way. They did not constitute a military establishment but rather a close-knit domestic force, always in attendance on the King, and maintained by him out of his private exchequer. A small force, admittedly, formed not by local gentry eager to defend their homes, but by ambitious young noblemen avid for places at court and proud to be near the King's person. Nevertheless, putting aside the question of motive on either side, Henry Tudor's Yeomen of the Guard were the descendants of those who fought by Harold's side in 1066 and the ancestors of the household troops of more modern times.

Henry VII laid the foundation of this new concept of civilian soldiers as the bulwark of the country's defence and gentlemen-at-arms as defenders of the King's person. The idea was developed by his son Henry VIII, who brought the country's militia to a high state of efficiency, employing, it must be admitted, coercive measures inconsistent with the tenets of free will and democracy. Three years after his accession an Act was passed laying down stringent rules aimed at stimulating the practice of archery by citizens, with butts set up on suitable land in all the principal towns and villages. Archery was a popular sport since it provided a means of competition among ordinary people, and it was popular, too, with the administration, because its steady practice improved the military value of the populace. Some years later, on August 25th 1537, the King granted a charter to the Master of the Ordnance of the Tower of London and two gentlemen of the Privy Chamber for a Fraternity "consisting of four masters or rulers and such brethren as they should admit", for promoting the "science of artillery". The term artillery in those days referred to long bows, cross-bows and hand-guns.

This Charter had historic consequences. It led to the formation of a Guild or Company which in unbroken development became what is known today as the Honourable Artillery Company, one of the most famous regiments in the British Army. The "Fraternity of the Guild of St. George", as it was known by the Charter of 1537, rapidly assumed a position of great importance in the military life of the nation. Among its most valued privileges were permission to shoot at game and fowl all over the Kingdom; and exemption from all criminal proceedings if, "after calling the word 'Fast' before shooting, anyone should be killed by passing between the shooter and the butt".

It is perhaps pertinent at this point to refer to the peculiar position of the H.A.C. in the hierarchy of the British military forces. In 1782 the members offered their services as a military body without pay, in defence of the Metropolis and its environs, but had no military rank assigned to them. "They are not of the Militia", Clode wrote in his "The Military Forces of the Crown" in 1869, "but of the Volunteer Force, and, as the oldest Corps, their place is on the right of the line". By Royal Warrant in 1849 the H.A.C. was recognised as a military organisation with its commissioned officers taking rank in the Army only during the time of the Company being on actual service. Despite Clode's observation it is a fact that the Honourable Artillery Company in 1863 was specifically excluded from the operation of the Volunteer Act of that year. It would seem, then, that the H.A.C. was in the peculiar position of being neither in the Regular Army, the Militia nor the Volunteers. What is certain is that it is the oldest surviving

Citizen soldiers of the Loyal Associated Ward Volunteer Corps of the
City of London, 1800

THE SOLDIER's FAREWELL.

To you, my dearest Nancy, I entrust my greatest charge—my children:—should I fall in the glorious cause, my family will receive succour from the fostering hand of my generous country.—I go to defend you all against the attacks of a daring Invader; one who threatens the shores of England with his desperate Legions: I go to preserve my wife and children from abject slavery.—Imprint in the minds of my boys, the deeds of their forefathers; teach them the history of Britannia's Heroes; tell them of Cressy's glorious field, when Edward raised his sable shield, and rushed to glory through an host of foes. The plains of Poictiers then shall be recorded, and Agincourt's tremendous Battle, when our Fifth Harry, with a Lion's heart, broke through the Gallic ranks, and lowered the pride of France!—Such are the deeds that lead to glorious emulation!—Ours is no common cause; we fight for our Liberty, our Religion, and our Laws, for every thing that is dear to our present existence, and also to posterity.—Dearest Nancy, adieu! the greater the danger, the more honor is to be gained:—in a short time I hope to return to you and my family, crowned with victorious laurels, torn from the brow of our insidious Foe. Then shall Peace and Plenty again visit our cottage, and happiness be the reward of virtue.—But hark! the trumpet sounds to arms—once more, Farewell!

'The Soldier's Farewell', typical of early nineteenth-century recruiting posters military organisation in the country with a record of faithful and distinguished service extending over five centuries right up to the present day.

Two years after giving his charter to the "Fraternity of St. George" the King, alarmed by the threat to the country by the proposed alliance between France and Spain, ordered extraordinary measures for defence against invasion. Castles and forts were built at strategic points on the coast, ship-building was pursued at a great pace, and the shire levy system entirely reorganised. Hitherto the sheriffs had had the responsibility for calling out the required levies. Now Henry appointed a distinguished gentlemen in each county to co-ordinate the recruiting and maintenance of the forces within its borders. These were the first lords-lieutenant, and we see in the statutes of those times a development of the idea of exploiting local enthusiasm and inculcating a spirit of county pride. Of course there was a degree of compulsion. Employers of labour were required at their own expense to furnish each able-bodied male between 17 and 60 with bows and other weapons, and practice at the butts was expected on high days and holidays. And in the end, assisted perhaps by the subjugation of the bow, hitherto the traditional English weapon and the yeoman's favourite, to newer and more complex weapons, the local enthusiasm for training and practice in arms gave place to a more general unwillingness to take on these duties, and a greater degree of evasion than was good for the country. For it seems that the county authorities, desperately trying to maintain the strengths of their respective forces, scoured the highways and the byways seeking recruits, who were ill-chosen and unfitted for any task but that of lowering the tone of each force and consequently affecting its efficiency and corrupting its morale.

The fact was that under the Tudors British love of action and a growing desire for conquest and colonisation of lands beyond the seas, to say nothing of the lure of rich prizes available on the seas themselves for adventurers brave enough to risk hardship and peril in search of them, had diverted the attention of many of our best and bravest men from the comparative humdrum routine of drills and practice at home. So it was that in the latter part of the reign of Henry VIII, throughout that of Mary, and for the first years of Elizabeth's long rule, the home forces deteriorated in many ways, and certainly in the counties and places outside the big towns and cities. In the large centres of population and trade civic pride and a greater awareness of the issues involved went a long way towards maintaining at least an adequate standard of competence. Particularly was this the case in London, and the marked efficiency of the trained bands of the capital was due not only to the Londoner's traditional independent spirit and loyalty but also to that "Guild of St. George" which Henry VIII had founded in 1537.

By this time the Guild had become established as the Artillery Company of London and the individual members of the corps were so practised in the soldierly arts, so keen, so devoted, that they had become the Tudor equivalent of a staff college. It was not surprising, therefore, that members of the H.A.C. should be deputed to act as training officers for the trained bands. The work was well done, with enthusiasm and efficiency, and when, in 1585, there was another threat of a Spanish Invasion, Elizabeth was able to call with confidence on the citizens of London to the defence of the capital.

A force of 4,000 men was recruited with members of the H.A.C. as officers. Three years later the trained bands of London, with their H.A.C. officers, were reviewed by Elizabeth at Tilbury, where they had mustered on the news that the Armada had sailed. That great and menacing fleet was, we know, thrown into confusion by the smaller and more manageable English vessels in the Channel, and finally dispersed and partly destroyed by storms. So the citizens of London were not required to fight in defence of their queen and their city; but there is little doubt that, prepared as probably no corps of part-time soldiers had ever been prepared before, they would have given a good account of themselves.

6

THE death of Elizabeth in 1603 meant more than the end of the Tudor dynasty. It began the decline of the free, individual and adventurous spirit which had made her reign glorious and productive. But the Stuart dynasty, although marked first by parsimony and meanness of character, later by extravagance and insincerity, and always by distorted and mal-adjusted politics at home and abroad, brought about a great change in the nature of the country's military forces. And this had an important influence on the conception of volunteer soldiering. Eleven years after his succession James I ordered the Lord Mayor of London to muster the spare-time forces of the City and form them into companies of trained bands. No doubt this was done by an apprehensive sovereign to ensure the protection of the City in time of trouble. But those same trained bands were to play an important part in the Civil War. In 1643 two regiments of the London trained bands and three regiments of auxiliaries marched to the relief of Gloucester, then beseiged by Charles I; and the same men subsequently fought in the first battle of Newbury. The importance of London in manpower can be judged from the fact that when the two regiments marched to Gloucester they left behind seven other regiments for the defence of the capital. At a general muster of London trained bands in September of the same year there were on the roll 18,064—including 7,200 auxiliaries. This muster was the last to concern the trained bands as such. As the ten years of Civil War proceeded the whole aspect of Britain's military forces changed, and when the bloodshed was over the country lay for the first time under the heel of a standing army.

But if the idea of spare-time soldiering implicit in the existence of trained bands had disappeared, the spirit of the volunteer lived on. During the Civil War there were great sacrifices on both sides by men unaccustomed to warfare but fired by enthusiasm for one cause or the other. On the declaration of the Commonwealth in May, 1649, the trained bands had disappeared into history and their place had been taken by the militia, a force organised on a semi-professional basis and forming in effect part of the Parliamentary Army.

Only a year passed before the unrest in Scotland which culminated in Montrose's abortive rebellion necessitated a strengthening of the defences of the chief towns so that regular soldiers could be released for the field. And in an order of Parliament dated August, 1650, we find a significant phrase. It provided for the furnishing of arms "to such London Volunteer Regiments" as needed them. The City Militia was also authorised to raise a troop of horse "at the expense of the inhabitants". If there were any doubt about the voluntary nature of these efforts they were dispelled by a letter from the Council of State to various militia commanders.

"It is not meant to impose this service on everybody," ran the letter, "but to leave it to every man's freedom, not doubting that the well-affected and able will be willing to put themselves in such a posture, by this voluntary listing, which will be of little or no charge to them, as may enable them both to serve the public and preserve themselves against the designs of the enemy."

The execution of Montrose and the success of the Cromwellian army in the Battle of Dunbar did not end the state of emergency, for in the following summer the invasion of England by Charles II brought renewed activity in the recruitment of volunteers. Major General Skippon, commander of the City of London troops, issued a call for volunteers and on August 12th the Council of State was authorised by Parliament to spend such money as was required for encouraging and paying persons voluntarily enlisting in "regiments of volunteers in and about London". Steps were also taken to raise troops of horse, and this pattern was repeated in all the big towns in the provinces. Commissions were given to local leaders for raising regiments of volunteers at key towns like Oxford, Hereford, Gloucester and Bristol, but it was emphasised that these additional forces were "not to expect pay".

Because the companies of foot soldiers were intended to replace professional regiments in the home garrison and neither these volunteers nor the troops of horse were to expect pay, except while on active service, it has been maintained that the companies raised in the 1650–51 emergency were intended as volunteer additions to the militia and therefore that their formation could not be regarded as a spontaneous origin of the volunteer movement. Surely this is an unnecessary and probably unjust distinction. Whether the companies in question were militia, auxiliary militia, or independent volunteers is beside the point. They volunteered out of patriotism and without consideration of possible pecuniary advantage. They were indeed no different from the official volunteers of later times who gave their services for similar reasons and had about the same prospects of remuneration. The status of the volunteers of 1650–51 was, I think, made clear when, following the Battle of Worcester and the flight of Charles II, which rapidly brought the country back to normal, the national militia was disbanded. The disbandment was effected by an Order in Council dated September 17th, but on the previous day an entirely separate Order had been issued disbanding "The Regiments of Volunteers of the City and parts adjacent ... accompanied by our good acceptance of their forwardness to appear at a time of such emergency".

If the volunteer regiments so described had been officially regarded as auxiliaries to the militia, the disbandment of the militia would have included them. But they were specifically provided for in a separate order and given the title "Volunteers".

There was, of course, no reason now to retain either militia or volunteers. Parliamentary Forces were supreme and more than adequate to cope with any situation, now that Charles II was abroad and the country settling down to existence as a Commonwealth. And the temper of the nation was fast turning against the continued existence even of the military power which had produced the Commonwealth and made the people of Britain free from royal tyranny. So it was not surprising for more than one reason that the restoration of the Stuarts in 1660 should be followed almost immediately by a general reduction in the armed forces. Economy was one over-riding reason, but another equally important was that the nation was heartily sick of soldiers.

The army which won the Civil War was no ordinary army. It had sprung from volunteer sources and was composed mainly of men who were not only full of intelligence, culture and quiet courage, but also actuated by the purest motives and following exacting rules of sobriety and morality. They had been recruited, to use Lord Macaulay's phrase, "not by the arts of the recruiting officers but by religious and political zeal."

"The boast of the soldiers," observed Macaulay, "as we find recorded in their solemn resolutions, was that they had not been forced into the service, nor had enlisted for the sake of the lucre; that they were not janissaries but free-born Englishmen, who had of their own accord put their lives in jeopardy for the liberties of religion in England, and whose right and duty it was to watch over the welfare of the nation they had saved".

Nevertheless, public opinion was against a permanent army. However much the Cromwellian soldiers had fought and suffered in the cause of liberty, however much they had achieved in creating a situation which would permit the restoration of the monarchy on more democratic lines, they were objects of annoyance to a population determined to make peace last and to enjoy it while it lasted. Charles II on his accession was bound to pay court to the popular wish for a democratic way of life, yet determined to preserve what he could of the powers of absolute monarchy. By one Act of Parliament he abolished the old system of knights' fees which had been introduced by the Assize of Arms more than five centuries earlier, and which was not only outdated as a means of recruitment but had become a corrupt engine for intrigue at Court. Another Act brought into being a militia remodelled to suit the new requirements of a democratic nation at peace. Every man with a capital of £6,000 or more, or an income from land of at least £500 a year, had to provide at his own charge one horseman. The individual with at least £50 from land or a capital of £600 or more was required to furnish one foot soldier, clothed, equipped and paid by himself.

Even less affluent inhabitants did not escape their obligations. They were formed into groups, each group providing a man or men according to the means available. The force thus raised, which varied between 100,000 and 150,000 men, was not to be compared with the tried Parliamentary troops or to the highly-trained and well-equipped armies of the Continental powers, but as a result of the Civil War it had a much greater level of efficiency than any of the part-time armies of earlier reigns. It satisfied a populace who were content that these men should appear occasionally for their drills, and not be always in evidence as representatives of oppression and discipline, as the soldiers of Cromwell had been for far too long.

Yet it was not possible to be entirely rid of the regular forces which the Civil War had brought into being. Charles II was very keen to have around his person and within easy call of his palace a force of tried, skilled and trained soldiers, officered by men he could trust, as a cushion against popular revolt. This force was formed of three troops of carabiniers each of 200 men—the original Life Guards. Most of the members of this force came from Cavalier families and the great majority had been officers in the royal army. Now they served as privates and N.C.O.s, but all without exception were known as the Gentlemen of the Guard. It was perhaps no coincidence that round about this time, in France, another king was gathering about him a guard of gentlemen who would defend him to the death; these were uneasy times for crowned heads.

The maintenance of Charles's small force, the Stuart equivalent of the Danish huscarles, was a charge on the royal exchequer, although the Commons had granted a yearly revenue of £1,200,000 on the understanding that this sum should not be used in any way for the maintenance of a permanent military force. The Gentlemen of the Guard, it is evident, were not placed in such a category, having regard to their small numbers and the personal nature of their duties. But the Commons also realised the danger of carrying through a complete disbandment of the army, and decided to retain in service two regiments—the Coldstream Guards and the Horse Guards. These, with ancillaries, made up a force of about 5,000 men which, by the end of Charles's reign, had grown to about 10,000, of which less than 2,000 were mounted. In these military moves of Charles and his Parliament we see not only the beginnings of a regular army, but also the origin of the Brigade of Guards.

The reconstitution of these forces meant a concentration of military power in London, and this was reinforced by the fact that when Charles II, soon after his accession, made an order disbanding the trained bands, he specifically expected those of London, which remained in being, and later became the City of London Militia. But the volunteer movement itself became dormant once more as Britain under the Restoration entered a quarter of a century of peace at home.

7

THE abolition of knights' fees by Charles II not only
marked the end of an outworn and outmoded method of
recruiting the nation's manpower for military purposes,
but also removed what had become a scandal. The effect of the
move was to acknowledge the fact that the government of the
country in the 17th century, under the influence of the changes
wrought by the Civil War, had been transformed from an
absolute monarchy responsible both for raising and remunerating
the armed forces into a limited monarchy under which the
defence of the nation was a matter of public organisation and
control, and the expense a charge on the public. In other words
the authority and the burden had passed from the Crown to the
Parliament. The knight's fee therefore had become an anachron-
ism; worse, it had led to corruption under the Stuarts which had
caused a great deal of misery and injustice. The knight's fee, or
fief, had been instituted by the Normans solely to provide a
feudal host for war purposes. But it developed into a barbarous
system by which every successive holder of a knight's fee had
to pay a part of his inheritance to the Crown on succeeding to his
patrimony. If the inheritor were a minor the Crown not only had
the right to enjoy the major part of the revenue, but also the rights
and the powers of guardianship during minority. This, in cases
where the inheritor was a female, could and did lead to corruption
and distress, since marriage to a ward of the Crown was added to
the gifts with which a king could placate a creditor or reward a
favourite. Of course all such powers had ended with the death of

Charles I, and it was in the natural order of things that it should not be revived under the Restoration.

All this was very much in tune with the mood of a nation sick of strife and ready to enjoy the supposed delights of a country not only at peace but also ruled by a monarch unfettered by and, indeed, opposed to, the puritanical notions and inhibitions of the Commonwealth régime. As the people had flocked to the standards of Roundhead and Cavalier, according to inclination or sentiment, so they now flocked to the maypole, the alehouse and the fair. Masculine rivalry found an outlet in sports and pastimes, and England presented a picture of peace and contentment, as it had done in Elizabethan times. On the Continent things were very different. There, with land frontiers to guard, the various nations had what, for those times, were great standing armies and vast fortifications well garrisoned. The peasant was constantly reminded of war by the sight of troops and often had cause to regret the presence of soldiery in his neighbourhood. But in England even the Civil War had left large parts of the country uncontaminated by military arrays or activities, and with the virtual disbandment of the Parliamentary forces it became an event, outside the big towns, to see a professional. Indeed, signs of warlike behaviour were to be seen only when the militia or trained bands turned out for their infrequent exercises and drills, and there were not wanting those who looked askance even at these comparatively mild exhibitions of military activity, and perhaps had contempt for men who could hardly be expected to match the professional soldiers which an aggressive Continental power might bring to English shores. In fact the militia were not regarded by some sections of the public so seriously as they regarded themselves, and John Dryden, who had fought on the Parliamentary side in the Civil War but was now Poet Laureate under Royal patronage, was biting in his contempt of the militia:

> The country rings around with loud alarms
> And raw in fields the rude militia swarms.
> Mouths without hands, maintained at vast expense,
> In peace a charge, in war a weak defence.

Stout once a month they march, a blustering band,
And ever, but in time of need, at hand.
This was the morn when, issuing on the guard,
Drawn up in rank and file they stood prepared
Of seeming arms to make a short assay,
Then hasten to be drunk, the business of the day.

Satirical poets went out of fashion, but there remained in many minds a secret contempt for or amused tolerance of part-time soldiers. In later centuries the Volunteers and the early Territorials were regarded in much the same light by the uninformed or unthinking populace; and even in the midst of the Second World War there were those who regarded the various Home Guard exercises in the countryside, culminating in beer and sandwiches in some village hostelry, in much the same way as Dryden regarded the militia of the Restoration.

Nevertheless, however the ignorant and untutored section of the population might regard the militia, it was popular with the country gentry, and not only because they were involved with it and supplied most of its officers. In their minds this national force was a safeguard against exploitation of the people by the Crown and an insurance against the establishment of a standing army. The militia under the Tudors and the early Stuarts was a much more important body than it had been under the Plantagenets or was to be under the Commonwealth. There was indeed a country-wide fervour for service and pride in the practice of arms which reached its peak, perhaps, at the time of the Armada. Then not only the citizens of London but the inhabitants of the provincial towns, the squires of the countryside and the yokels of the villages, rallied to the national cause. All round the coast the beacons were built and guarded; in all the seaports fortifications were garrisoned, and fishermen and longshoremen vied with farmers and labourers in expressing loyalty to the Crown and defiance of the enemy. Perhaps a great deal of this enthusiasm sprang from the knowledge that the ordinary citizen represented the military might of the nation. There was no regular army, there were no household troops beyond a few Gentlemen of the

Guard, and the armed populace could be equally powerful in reaction against oppression and tyranny as in support of a wise and benevolent monarchy. It was often easier for a rebel to raise an army of insurrection than for the Government to muster forces for a legitimate object. For this reason even popular kings had to move warily lest they infringed the rights of their subjects.

So, for many years, the armed might of the people represented the military power of the country. This power, during the years of the Civil War, was channelled into Roundhead and Cavalier forces, but after the Restoration the militia again became important. In fact, with the reduction of the Parliamentary forces to a few regiments the growth of the militia was almost automatic, and indeed essential if Britain were to remain free from military domination. And when James II came to the throne and tried to develop a strong standing army the militia very quickly resumed its former status.

In 1685, when Charles II died, the units of the Parliamentary forces kept in commission at the Restoration had grown into a regular army of nearly ten thousand men. About a fifth of these were mounted, and the whole cost more than a quarter of a million a year. James was very keen to increase the size of this force, and the Monmouth rebellion was soon to give him the opportunity of doing so in defiance of popular opinion against any extension of the Royal forces. The whole sorry business of Monmouth—how he was led to false estimates of the support he might get in England, how he was joined by the ignorant, unthinking and ill-armed yokels of the West Country but virtually ignored by the gentry, how he and his advisers mismanaged the invasion and their subsequent movements; how he was beaten at Sedgemoor and finally paid for his temerity on the scaffold, has been told many times. Less attention has been paid to the part played by the militia in this short campaign.

When an event like the Monmouth rebellion occurs there are bound to be divided loyalties, and the part-time soldiers of England differed in their allegiances according to circumstances and inclinations, just as they had separated into Roundheads and Cavaliers at the start of the Civil War. For example, the Duke of

Albemarle, at the time of Monmouth's advance from Lyme Regis happened to be reviewing 4,000 of the Devon militia. He was Lord-Lieutenant of the county, a son of General Monk and loyal to the Crown. But his men showed such signs of disaffection and unwillingness to fight for King James that he deemed it wiser to withdraw them from contact with Monmouth's forces rather than risk an engagement which might damage the prospects of the Royal arms. Fortunately for James and unfortunately for Monmouth the militia of the West Country for the most part remained loyal to the Crown. The Devon men further West were apparently reliable. Wiltshire militia had mustered in strength under the Earl of Pembroke, who had no qualms about their behaviour. But the most effective movement was in Gloucestershire. The Duke of Beaufort, Lord-Lieutenant of that county and also of Somerset, Monmouthshire and Herefordshire, mustered all available forces and set up an elaborate defence of the City of Bristol—a strategic action which was to have a decisive influence on the fortunes of Monmouth.

Nearer London the City of Oxford and the University students were all strongly for the King, and so all along the line the part-time defenders were in action while, back in Whitehall, the King and his advisers were planning the disposition of the regular forces. These were under the command of Lord Faversham, and the officer in command of the Blues was Lt. John Churchill, whose performance in this short campaign foreshadowed the glorious triumphs of his prime.

Despite the mustering of the militia of the shires there was much distrust in James's mind about their loyalty, and he seized the opportunity afforded by the crisis to step up the strength of the regular army. One of the new regiments formed at this time was destined to play a long and honourable role in realms far beyond London, the city of its birth. This was the Royal Regiment of Fusiliers, so called from the fact that the soldiers were armed with a wide-bore musket termed a fusil. This regiment, formed to guard the Tower of London and so release other troops for duties in the field, was perpetuated in the history of the British Army as the Royal Fusiliers (City of London Regiment), and eventually absorbed the Royal London Militia, which became the 7th Battn. Royal Fusiliers. This was one of the earliest examples of a Regiment of the Line taking under its wing a regiment of part-time soldiers. Much later in its career, in 1940 and after the Fusiliers had won battle honours in many lands, part-time soldiers wore the "fusil" crest. They were the City of London Home Guard.

But James and his ministers were not content with the forma-tion of an odd regiment or two. They were bent on expanding the existing regiments as well, and by the end of the Monmouth adventure the number of regular troops had been increased three-fold. James now had more than 20,000 men permanently under arms and would have liked more. But with the end of the emer-gency he ran up against traditional popular antagonism. The King had against him not only the general public, with memories of the tyranny of the Parliamentary forces and fears of free billeting and other evils, but also the landowners and gentry of the counties, who had no wish to see their prerogatives as officers and petty rulers of the militia overshadowed by the power and importance of a large array of household troops and permanent military camps. There were hot debates in Parliament, and in spite of threats and intrigues James could not obtain by constitu-tional means sufficient money for his ends. Indeed the Commons only reluctantly voted him half what he asked, and so precipitated a constitutional crisis. Later, as his relations with Parliament and populace worsened, James made what show he could by assembl-ing all his available forces and forming a great camp of more than 12,000 men on Hounslow Heath. But that was all he could do, and he would have been well advised not to attempt even that. The Parliamentary policy was clear—to limit money spent on regular forces and concentrate on modernising and re-organising the long discredited militia.

8

JAMES the Second did not get his standing army. In view of what happened towards the close of his reign such an army would have been of little use to him. But Parliament, having resisted his efforts, found it easy to write safeguards into their agreement with William of Orange when he accepted the throne on behalf of himself and his wife Mary, daughter of James II. Scarcely a month after the accession of William and Mary the fugitive Stuart king invaded Ireland with the assistance of French forces, and there were fears of a French invasion of the South Coast of England. Regular troops were posted at various key positions, with a concentration of seasoned troops in and around Portsmouth, and there was a great review of some 13,000 men of the London regiments of volunteers—those regiments which had not been included in the general disbandment of the trained bands after the accession of Charles II.

The Bill of Rights enacted by William soon after his accession established in no uncertain terms the illegality of a standing army in time of peace, unless instituted by authority of Parliament. The only justification for a regular army, it was laid down, would be the need to preserve the balance of power abroad. The Bill of Rights, by its contents and the very fact of its presence on the Statute Book, proved that the days of Divine Right and Absolute Monarchy were dead. Henceforth any monarch who occupied the throne of England would be subject to Parliament for the necessary supplies and answerable to the people for all his actions. Yet, paradoxically, whereas James II, without such an enactment, was thwarted in his desire for a standing army; William III, after the Bill had been passed, did obtain what James had failed to get. The difference was that whereas James II wanted a standing army to oppress his people and bring them under the subjection of France and the Roman Catholic Church, William III wanted one to defend his people and resist foreign machinations, including, of course, the French support of James's cause. Another difference, and an important one, was that the standing army which William commanded was formed by permission and under the control of Parliament.

The Peace of Ryswick, which ended the war between England and France, left England with a regular army of close on 100,000 men, mostly all seasoned campaigners, and there were actually those who, with bitter memories of oppression and injustice under the Commonwealth and the Stuarts, desired nothing less than the total disbandment of these forces. The idea, of course, was sheer nonsense. The world had moved into the realm of power politics. Britain was no longer an island whose only task was to repel invaders. Politically the nation had become part of the Continent of Europe and the latest peace treaty was to be but a temporary halt in the diplomatic game now being played by the European powers, and destined to go on in ever increasing complexity. So although there were advocates of a return to a modest establishment of regular troops and a reliance on the militia as the main source of manpower in emergency, the situation demanded the maintenance under arms of a strong professional army. The militia, it must be remembered, was by no means so large a body, in proportion to the population, as the fyrd had been in Anglo-Saxon times. It had declined in size and effectiveness under Elizabeth, and when James I ordered a national roll-call on succeeding to the throne in 1603, the total of available manpower was about 23,000, of whom roughly a third were horsemen. When Charles II organised a regular army in 1660 he reconstituted the militia in such a way that it became even more than hitherto a part-time force with limited and infrequent duties. Those called were not required to serve outside the kingdom, the various companies had only four musters a year and the county regiments only one a year. It may be argued that a force of this kind would have been hard pressed to keep the peace among the inhabitants of the country, would have fared ill in any clash with numberous well-armed and well-led invaders, and was likely to be of little use in service alongside seasoned regulars.

It was small wonder, therefore, that individual cities and towns should look askance at the existing militia and take steps to ensure a better defensive system. In 1649 the Council of State had authorised the formation of a company of volunteers in Birmingham "for the safety of the county", and developments of this kind occurred in several parts of the country in Stuart times until the Civil War led to a tremendous change in emphasis. From those years onwards the militia was subject to two pressures— the institution and apparent permanence of a regular army which considerably lessened the importance of the militia; and the gradual emergence of another type of part-time soldier, the true volunteer. For a great number of years, until well into the 18th century, the diminishing status of the militia, combined with a growing unwillingness to serve in it and a parallel growth of enthusiasm for volunteering, tended to make the national force in post-Stuart days like the fyrd after the Norman Conquest—outmoded and largely unwanted.

The increasing importance of spontaneous and impromptu volunteering was seen in 1690 after the victory of the French fleet over the English and Dutch fleets off Beachy Head. There were grave fears that the French were about to land on the coast near Torbay. In twenty-four hours, stated a contemporary account, the whole of Devon was mobilised. The beacons blazed on the promontories and the yeomen of the county, led by the squires and landed gentry, prepared to resist to the utmost.

Such ardour was most usefully channelled into the right course by the formation of volunteer units, some highly unofficial, others formed with the permission of the blessing of authority so long as the members carried on their activities at their own expense and therefore did not become a charge on the community. These units were formed and fell into disuse, flourished or waned according to circumstances, for years afterwards until the middle of the 19th century when the Volunteer Force was placed on a permanent footing. It is true, as Sebag-Montifiore has pointed out in his "History of the Volunteer Force", that the Volunteer Force was not the creation of any particular year or century or period. It was a natural development of the plain Englishman's realisation of his responsibilities towards his King and his Country, which had been so often expressed, in so many different ways, over the centuries. What made the volunteer grow in importance in Hanoverian times was the diminishing reputation and status of the militia. Among the many reasons for this change was the fact that between the successful termination of William's campaign in Ireland and the Jacobite rising of 1745 there had been peace in these islands, and the regular army had been almost constantly employed abroad. The militia, in fact, had not been called upon for active service for nearly half-a-century when the '45 rebellion began, and ten years before then the Act authorising the organisation and control of the militia by the counties had been allowed to lapse. Indeed, the country would have been in a sorry state if Bonnie Prince Charlie had had only the local militia to contend with, for the situation in manpower and arms, bad all over the country, was nowhere worse than in the North-West of England, where the Jacobite forces were allowed to progress almost unimpeded to Derby. A survey carried out by Sir George Oxenden some years before had revealed these facts:

Cumberland and Westmorland: Only 600 men in the whole area and arms "extremely bad". Carlisle (which was to fall so easily to the Young Pretender) had 20 cannon to protect weak walls, and only two companies of foot and one troop of horse.

Lancashire. In the whole county only three regiments of foot, only one officer who knew how to form a company, and "no man trained or exercised since King William's time".

Chester Castle: Defended by 75 men (all time-expired veterans) and no ammunition or stores.

Durham Castle. Without arms and ammunition.

In the Southern Counties things were not much better. The 46 guns of Pendennis Castle, commanding Falmouth Harbour, were in charge of a master gunner 90 years old and one assistant. There were similar reports from Sandown, Rochester and other important forts.

It was in these circumstances, with the militia in a sorry state of unpreparedness, and with the regular forces below strength, that a haphazard form of volunteering came to the rescue. County leaders were given a free hand, even encouraged, to raise loyal bodies both foot and mounted, and all over the country squires and lords of the manor, as well as respectable burgesses and leading professional men in the towns, were given commissions for this purpose. The call went out from parish halls for volunteers and men flocked to sign attestation sheets called "Associations for Defence". The title stuck, as we can see down to the present day in the existence of Territorial Associations in the various counties.

The enthusiasm was widespread. One of the first Associations, if not the first, was formed in Northamptonshire in April, 1744, in face of the threat of a French invasion in support of the Jacobite claims to the throne. The Duke of Montagu, Lord-Lieutenant of Northants, soon obtained the signatures of 530 "substantial freeholders, yeomen, and the sons of yeomen". He expressed the intention of forming them into troops according to their various localities and to appoint "those of the best estate among them" to be commanders. It was an age of privilege and the day of the ranker-officer had yet to dawn! With great pride the noble Duke was able to assure the government that in the hour of peril they could call on a body of 500 men "more to be depended upon than the militia". His reason for this claim was that the volunteers were actuated entirely by goodwill towards and zeal for King and government, whereas the militia "consist of the dis-affected as well as the well-affected". Such criticism of the older body was no doubt justified because the difficulties of recruitment had led to the absorption into the militia of many unsuitable and unreliable characters whose loyalties must always have been suspect.

The full text of the Association of Northamptonshire, dated April 4th, 1744, and to be found in the State Papers, runs:

"We whose names are underwritten do humbly desire that we may be permitted to form ourselves into a body to fight in defence of His Majesty's Crown, the Protestant Religion and the Liberties of Great Britain against Popery and Slavery, under the command of his Grace the Duke of Montagu as our Captain and such other officers as he may appoint. And we engage each of us to mount ourselves upon our own horses and to cloath (*sic*) ourselves in uniform cloaths at our own expense. And to be ready when called upon by our Captain to serve within our realm, wherever His Majesty's services shall require, upon our being paid Trooper's Pay during the time we shall be employed, and being paid for our horses if lost in the service."

This Northants Association of horsemen had other claims to distinction besides the fact that it was probably the progenitor of the Yeomanry Regiments. It was the first volunteer body of any kind which specifically widened its area of service to embrace any part of the realm to which the King's Service might call its members. Many county Associations were formed subsequently and during the next two years, but none had so wide a scope as the Northamptonshire Yeomanry, and the great majority restricted their promised activities to their own particular regions. One Regiment of Light Horse (later called the Royal Regiment of Horse) was formed in 1745 "to harass the rebels in their march, give intelligence of their motions to the King's forces, and to remove everything that may be of service to the enemy". The scorched earth policy at birth. On the other hand, after France had declared war in 1744, a body calling themselves the "Gentlemen Volunteers of London" expressed themselves "ready and willing to march against the Pretender, his adherents, or any invader, *wherever the foot guards shall march within Great Britain*". They further gave assurance that they would do so at no expense to the Government except for pay for the officers.

But whether restricted or unrestricted as to area, the various Associations were animated by the same sense of loyalty and consideration of duty. Sir George Oxenden, whose survey of the country's defences had revealed so much that was wanting, made himself responsible for rallying volunteers in Kent and rapidly assembled a force of 1,500 men, armed and provisioned, ready to defend whatever part of the south coast might be attacked by the

French. There was a fine response in other counties, and seamen and fishermen offered their services in great numbers. There was an "Association", signed by nearly 1,000 smugglers, in response to a suggestion that these gentlemen of the hooded lights and the packhorses, with their intimate knowledge of coastline and coastal ways, might be just as effective in keeping out French sailors as they had been in getting in French brandy.

These and many other activities in the new volunteer movement went on, and the country was ready as it never had been before when, in the summer of 1745 the Young Pretender, without French support and with only lukewarm backing by the majority of Highland chiefs, but encouraged by his victory at Prestonpans and his partial success at Edinburgh, began his invasion of England. The capitulation of Carlisle after only a week of siege was not followed by the hoped-for Jacobite risings in the Northern counties, and the Pretender's progress petered out at Derby. There followed the retreat, the wastage of his little army, its final extinction at Culloden, and Charles Edward's escape overseas.

It was now April, 1746, just two years since the 500 Northamptonshire horsemen had signed their "Association". There was no longer any danger from without, and therefore no cause for further expressions of loyalty within. A few months later the Associations born with so much enthusiasm in a time of crisis were officially disbanded with the King's personal thanks. The volunteer movement had for the time being served its purpose. More than a hundred years were to pass before it became a permanent and self-contained feature of our national life. Nevertheless, despite the hasty disbandment of 1746, the need for an overhaul of the part-time forces of the country remained, and this became intensified during the next decade, owing to the political situation consequent on the reverses suffered by British arms at the hands of the French. A considerable reform of the military structure of the country was begun by William Pitt, later Earl Chatham, and the two Acts of Parliament by which this was achieved represented an important stage in the evolution of the volunteer movement, since for the first time there was official recognition of the fact that the volunteer force and the militia were separate entities.

But these reforms were not achieved without difficulty, both at Westminster and in the country at large. The struggle began in 1755 when The Hon. George Townsend proposed in the House of Commons an investigation into the militia laws to maintain, as he put it, the virtues of a citizen army "dear to the heart of every patriotic Englishman". Pitt thereupon prepared and introduced a Bill providing for a militia of up to 60,000 men to be kept on a permanent footing with a set number of drill days (as many as 110 in a year) and with a free issue of uniforms, pay on exercise days, and the services of adjutants and sergeants seconded from the Regular Army. The cost was estimated at £300,000 per year, and it was no doubt this fact and a certain amount of opposition from the landed gentry which led the Lords to reject the Bill after it had been passed by the Commons. This reverse delayed the reforms earnestly sought by Pitt, and made him so determined to have his way that he made the acceptance of this Bill by the Lords a condition of his becoming Secretary of State for War.

The Bill, as re-introduced under this arrangement, was the Militia Act of 1757 and one of its purposes was to take responsibility for raising, organising and maintaining the militia out of the hands of the provincial gentry and place it under the control of local government. Hitherto recruitment had been, to say the least, haphazard, with many loopholes and opportunities created by favouritism and nepotism. Henceforth, it was hoped, the net would be cast so wide that none would escape it. To accomplish this object lists were to be made of all available men between 18 and 50, first by districts, then by parishes and finally by counties. Those exempt from the ballot were peers, members of parliament, clergymen, constables, apprentices, seamen and any who could establish proper grounds for exemption, including physical incapacity, hardship, etc. The Lord-Lieutenant of each county was to have the task of deciding such claims, and every man declared eligible and selected by the ballot was to serve for three years under pain of a fine, unless he provided a suitable substitute.

The conditions of service were severe, much more so than

under former Acts. No longer would the militiaman be able to avoid the responsibility of being called to service. The programme of training was, indeed, a considerable burden on the ordinary citizen, and those involved were not slow to demonstrate reluctance to accept such onerous duties, which were regarded as bearing heavily on men who had to work long hours at the bench or in the fields while following their normal employment. Every month, except the four winter months, the militia were to have one-day exercises in half-companies and there was to be a company muster twice a year. In addition there were regimental assemblies at Easter and Whitsun, lasting three or four days each time, and other one-day drills on selected holidays. Drills were to last six hours a day. The men were not expected to go more than six miles from home for the four-day assemblies, but billeting was to be arranged where necessary at a cost (including food and small beer) of 1s. per officer and 4d. per man per day.

The 1757 Bill not only introduced the ballot system but also took control of the militia out of the hands of local landowners and made it the responsibility of the community. These circumstances, and the onerous nature of the training, created in the minds of the common people the idea that there was great inequality of sacrifice. This fact, together with dislike of the ballot and a measure of general unrest because of the continual rise in the price of corn, led to much disaffection which broke out into rioting in many parts of the country. Some malcontents, armed with clubs, scythes and pitchforks for want of other weapons, went so far as to wreck buildings where the ballots were held, destroying ballot papers and assaulting and insulting officials. These disturbances were put down only with difficulty and not until some sentences of deportation and, in two or three cases, hanging had been passed was it possible to proceed smoothly with the procedure laid down by the Act. It was passed by the Lords only after a number of amendments, including a reduction of the establishment to 32,000 officers and men, had been grudgingly conceded by Pitt.

The new Act laid down a quota of three officers to every eighty men, and with a three-year rota of service it was hoped to achieve in time a sizeable reserve of manpower, reasonably well trained, to be called on in an emergency. But one difficulty was a great shortage of officers, and in some counties several months passed before the necessary appointments were made. Not surprisingly the biggest county contribution to the militia quota came from Yorkshire to the number of 2,360 or just over 7 per cent. of the national total. Yorkshire also had the distinction of providing the first regiment to be raised under this Act. It was Colonel Thornton's Regiment (later the 3rd West York Light Infantry) and although several meetings had to be held before the list of officers was complete, these commissions were granted by the King on January, 27th, 1759. In the following September, by which time many regiments had been formed in England and Wales, the new militia was officially embodied.

Public discontent with the ballot system and the severe training conditions had been accompanied by annoyance among the middle classes and the landed classes at the arbitrary character of the Act. Those who did not wish to serve in any capacity were against service as such. Those who welcomed the idea of serving King and Country in time of peril were opposed to inclusion in a ballot. It may be judged therefore what an enthusiastic reception was given to an Act of 1758 which authorised companies of militia to incorporate in their ranks any who offered themselves as volunteers. These men had to accept all the conditions of service applying to militiamen, but they were excused the ballot and so could claim to be true volunteers and not pressed men.

The war with France had reached such a stage in May, 1759, that the King, in a message to the Commons, announced his intention of "marching the militia as occasion shall require", suggesting the likelihood of militia detachments being despatched to places not only outside their own counties but also, perhaps, to places abroad. This did nothing, of course, to dispel public disquiet at what was regarded as illegal use of the militia. Some time earlier there had been instances of men being transferred from the militia into regular units and sent abroad. There were, of course, many volunteers in the militia who were only too ready to go anywhere and fight. But both the enthusiasm and the disquiet were misplaced. The militia were not required to fight the French, but they did fulfil a purpose in providing defences for the home front, maintaining public order and guarding prisoners of war. And it was a proud moment for many of them when, on 17th July 1759, the King reviewed the London Militia in Hyde Park. Three years later the Seven Years' War with France ended, and by the time the Treaty of Paris had been signed on 10th February 1763, the militia had been completely disembodied. The last regiment to stand down, at the end of January, was the 3rd Devon Regiment, and this, like many other English and Welsh regiments still in being, owed its origin to Pitt and the Seven Years' War.

Ten years later we had the Boston Tea-Party and before long Britain faced another crisis as the conflict with the American colonists developed into the War of Independence. And, following the familiar pattern, this crisis made possible another step in the evolution of the volunteer soldier. Lord North, Britain's Prime Minister, introduced in 1778 an Act authorising militia commanders to accept volunteers either to be incorporated into the militia companies as before, or to be formed into quite separate volunteer companies. For the first time an official distinction was made between a militia company formed by men directed by ballot and one consisting entirely of men freely and voluntarily offering their services. This move, of course, was highly popular, and in a very short time militia commanders all over the country were overwhelmed with requests to form volunteer companies. One regiment had no fewer than fourteen such companies attached to it within a year of the passing of the Act. There followed in 1779 an even more interesting event. A Bill was before Parliament aimed at doubling the militia to 60,000 men, and so many members of both parties showed so much favour towards the volunteers and the manner in which they had answered the call, that Lord North and his advisers recast the Bill. They abandoned the idea of doubling the militia and instead introduced a new Bill which duly became law and provided for a considerable increase in the volunteer force. The effect was the same as planned in the original measure, because about 30,000 men, as volunteers, were added to the existing militia force of about 30,000. The exact figures at the end of 1779, as given in Hay's "Constitutional Forces", showed that 62,780 men were on the strength of all militia establishments, of whom 30,740 were enrolled in volunteer companies.

The country and Parliament had, in fact, accepted the voluntary principle wholeheartedly, and this was reflected in the next Act concerning volunteers. It was designed to encourage and provide facilities for companies voluntarily enrolling for defence, even to the extent of planning volunteer battalions quite separate from other units, with pay and pension rights when called to active service. So now, it seemed, the volunteer was at last in a class of his own, independent of the militia and the Regular Army, giving his services from the strongest possible motives. It was just at this point, when there were prospects that volunteer soldiering would develop into a permanent movement and so derive strength from continuity, that the end of another crisis came to dash these hopes. There was, in fact, no time to put this act of 1782 into operation. In November of that year the American War of Independence ended in victory for the colonists, and in the following January the Treaty of Versailles apparently restored peace in Europe. There was no longer a need for part-time soldiers, and such volunteer companies and battalions that had been raised were abandoned. It was a repetition of the familiar pattern, and Britain had to wait for another threat from abroad before there could be further encouragement for the volunteer principle.

9

ANOTHER decade passed, and once more Britain was embroiled in war with the traditional enemy, France—now the France of Napoleon. And again the onset of hostilities and the threat of invasion found us ill-prepared—a situation not unfamiliar to Englishmen and one which was to recur several times afterwards. If in the 20th century we had not learned the lessons of unpreparedness, we were certainly in the elementary stages of education in the closing years of the 18th. There had been no lack of examples for the folly of neglect, but no rush to profit by past mistakes. The Militia Acts of 1782–3 had been in force for ten years and the state of the militia was little better than that which those Acts had been introduced to improve. In fact the substitute system had been abused to such an extent that the militia had recruited by this means men who might have joined the regular army; and the Navy press gangs had still further affected enlistment for the land forces.

If the state of the country militarily was unsatisfactory it must be written that on the credit side the enthusiasm of the nation's manhood for rallying to action adjusted the balance. Once again spontaneous activities of this kind were ahead of Government action. In March, 1794, inhabitants of the West End of London formed an Association for the Parish of St. George's, Hanover Square, and very shortly five companies were in commission and ready to deal, as they did, with certain seditious activities in the capital. A few weeks later an Act was passed empowering counties and cities to raise volunteer bodies for local defence and, if need be, for national defence. Under these regulations many infantry regiments of volunteers, on the lines of the Hanover Square Association, were formed, and also, of course, many troops of volunteer horse. This was the signal for the revival of the Light Horse Volunteers of London—or rather a resumption of activity. Although this force had been technically disbanded in 1783 the members had agreed to keep in contact with a view to revival in the case of any ensuing emergency. And the war with Napoleonic France had barely begun when the London Light Horse were in being again to the extent of some 300 men.

The first Act of 1794 referring to volunteers authorised their enrolment in the militia battalions, with a bounty of £10 for every man so enrolled. But later the same year another Act was passed which had the same object as the abortive second Act of 1782; i.e., the formation of volunteer companies and battalions distinct from the militia. The urgency was real. Most of our regular troops were abroad fighting in the cause of the Allies, and it had become of paramount importance to strengthen the defences on the home front in preparation for possible invasion. The second Act of 1794 specifically exempted volunteers from liability to serve in the militia if they could prove adequate attendance at drills and training exercises of the corps to which they belonged.

But an even more significant reform was that counties were to be allowed to choose whether they would raise their forces by the militia ballot or by purely voluntary enlistment. Needless to say many county notables seized this chance to further the interests of the volunteer movement. It was another stage in the decline and fall of the national militia as the country's principal part-time force. The recruitment of volunteers under the two acts of 1794 was accelerated by the fact that the Government, realising the seriousness of the situation and probably believing that the volunteers would in all probability be on active service, decided upon a scheme of pay and allowances which could not fail to be an additional inducement. Many volunteer corps had of course been formed with no thought of remuneration, and in some cases there were specific rejections of money payments. Some volunteers were financially independent. Others were in corps raised and maintained by wealthy landowners or burgesses who equipped officers and men in their own style and were content to be "different" even at considerable expense. But in general the monetary provisions of the 1794 Acts were accepted with thankfulness.

During the next three or four years, while operations were in progress on the Continent, several events occurred which increased the public alarm and intensified Government efforts to achieve complete mobilisation of the nation's manpower. There was, for example, the attempted invasion of Southern Ireland by a French fleet under Admiral Grouchy in 1796. The Irish landowners, mostly Protestant, were naturally alarmed and sought authority to organise local defence. The Government, after some understandable reluctance to the introduction of independent armed forces in Ireland, made the necessary Order and very quickly more than 100 troops of yeomanry were formed. Their services were not required, the French attempt failing partly through Grouchy's caution and finally because of a break-up of the weather. But the danger had been there and the local reaction typical.

In the following year the French made another attempt on the British Isles and this time effected an actual landing. The occasion had its humorous side, but it was indeed the only occasion on which volunteer corps had played a physical part in resisting an enemy landing in Great Britain. Three years earlier, under the 1794 Act, the Castlemartin Yeomanry Cavalry, later to become the Pembrokeshire Yeomanry, had been raised by Lord Cawdor as part of the volunteer movement in that Welsh county. A system for rapid mustering of the widely-scattered members of the corps had been worked out and this was put to the test, which it triumphantly survived, in February 1797, when a force of 1,400 French sailors and marines were landed at Llanwrda, near Fishguard, from three frigates. These enemy vessels had previously entered Torbay and made a call at Ilfracombe where they sank some merchant ships. But the French did not land there, putting out to sea before the North Devon volunteers under Colonel Orchard of Hartland Abbey could reach the coast.

At Llanwrda the French did effect a landing much to the consternation of all in the vicinity. The invaders were said to be ill-trained and rough men—"the sweepings of prisons and galleys"—and, having landed at night, they set about the task for which they were most fitted—looting and destruction. The fishermen and farm labourers of the district, grabbing whatever weapons they could find, put up some resistance and when day dawned the marauders found themselves opposed by a considerable force, consisting of the Castlemartin Yeomanry, some local militiamen, some sailors from a man-o-war then in Fishguard harbour, and various other parties. Lord Cawdor, apprised at midnight of this enemy invasion, had spent the next few hours mustering the defenders, and they must have made a more impressive show than a description of them would appear to indicate, because a reconnaissance in force was followed by the enemy requesting a truce. Lord Cawdor insisted on unconditional surrender, and the French actually complied and laid down their arms to a force which, as they then discovered, they outnumbered two to one.

There is no doubt the Castlemartin Yeomanry would have acquitted themselves well in any fight which might have resulted from this confrontation. It was a victory of bluff, but nevertheless a victory, and as such is entitled to a prominent place in the annals of the volunteer movement.

Such events as these, and weaknesses on the home front like the Spithead mutiny later the same year, increased public concern at the dangerous situation of the nation. And the inevitable Government reaction was to stimulate still further recruitment to the military forces, particularly the volunteers and the militia. This time the effort was wider in scope than any previous legislation of the kind. Indeed an Act of 1798 represented the first occasion in history on which the civilian population were enrolled for non-combatant as well as combatant services. The Act, as the preamble stated, was for the purpose of using, "in the most expeditious manner and with the greatest effect", the voluntary services of the King's loyal subjects. Lord Dundas (the War

Minister) expressed himself as anxious to give as much scope as possible for local and individual interpretations of the services required, and to give full latitude to the zeal of loyal men "to act in the mode most consistent with their own disposition and public spirit".

To this end returns, as usual, were required from the counties of all able-bodied men between 15 and 60—an extension of the former age limits 18–50—but the Lords-Lieutenant were also requested to state what service each man would be able to give. The returns had to include all classes of men under their various occupations. What William Pitt the Younger and Lord Dundas had done between them was to produce the kind of situation with which the country was to become familiar in the great wars of the 20th century—the involvement of the civilian in the war effort. A place had been found for the non-combatant. War was no longer waged only by professionals on a foreign field. It was coming home to everyone.

Another important difference between the 1798 Act and its predecessors was that control had been taken out of the hands of mayors and magistrates and put into the hands of the people—a democratic touch possibly ahead of its time but nevertheless calculated to stimulate public enthusiasm. The "Armed Associations" visualised by the Act were to be administered by committees elected by all the householders of each community, and officered by men elected by ballot. Each district of a parish was to have a company of fifty men, who would find their own uniforms but be armed and supplied by the Government. The officer commanding each Association was to arrange drills and duties, draw up orders for mustering in the event of fire at night and make other provisions for the welfare of his men and the safety of the community. Householders unable or not wishing to bear arms were employed within the Association as special constables and there was even enrolment of persons who, "though precluded by age or other cause from bearing arms or taking an active part, were desirous of joining solely with a view to promoting the interests and general purposes of the Association". Britain was indeed a nation mobilised for war.

One significant change in emphasis which we can trace to the 1798 Act was that it tended to break down class distinctions and extend the brotherhood of the volunteers throughout the population, irrespective of rank and occupation. For many years many of the volunteer corps had been formed mainly by persons in one class or calling, and were really military clubs associated with distinct professions or stations in society. These distinctions had been guarded jealously, so much so that in one instance the Gentlemen Volunteers of Exeter were actually disbanded in 1745 by the Mayor because they refused to be amalgamated with paid companies formed from among the local apprentices and mechanics. But in 1798 the general feeling was very different. The Bloomsbury Inns of Court Association in London, for example, was formed by lawyers for lawyers, but in the interests of emergency they not only formed an attached company of tradesmen and apprentices, but also contributed to their clothing and equipment. The Armed Associations of 1798 did indeed bring together the various sections of the population in the common cause. One of the specific objects of the Act was to create a force of both armed and unarmed men, the latter to be employed in various ways, including the evacuation to safety of women, children, old people and invalids, the removal of cattle and other movable property out of the enemy's reach and the destruction of property likely to be of use to him. There was, after all, only a difference of time and degree between the aims of Dundas and Pitt in 1798 and the exhortations of Churchill and Eden nearly a century and a half later. The extent of public support was very comforting to the Government, as all sections of the community answered the call. Fishermen and boatmen volunteered to man coastal defences in any emergency, and the humblest labourer seemed anxious to do what he could. These expressions of loyalty, together with a welcome increase in recruiting for the regular army, encouraged the Government to limit so far as possible the liability of locally-formed volunteer companies to serve away from their districts. It was ordained that only in the event of a special emergency or actual appearance of an enemy upon the coasts would extended service be required of any corps, and not even then if their presence within their respective districts should be deemed necessary for the preservation of tranquillity and the safety of their own homes. At the same time, to avoid an undue proportion of volunteers joining purely for the purpose of avoiding service in the militia, it was stipulated that if any offer of service were confined to the man's parish he could claim neither pay, grants for clothing, nor exemption from the militia. If, on the other hand, he consented to serve in the military district around his parish, he could get full allowances and also exemption. It will be seen that the Act effectively solved the problems of poor recruitment for the Army and widespread evasion of militia service, by extending the area in which volunteers would operate and so gaining the desired contribution to the mobile military strength of the country. And by the following March the Government was able to decree that volunteer corps "of all descriptions" be given relief from the ballots for the militia and the supplementary militia.

The situation was well described by a writer in *The British Volunteer* later that year: "Thus do we behold the nobleman, the statesman, the private gentleman and the mechanic co-operate without distinction in the common cause." He was referring to the fact that the Pimlico Volunteer Association included not only Members of Parliament and distinguished residents in Westminster but also the ordinary citizens of the district.

Understandably there was some reluctance on the part of the Army authorities to give volunteers any scope at all in artillery exercises. It was all very well to entrust these part-time, part-trained men with small arms, but ordnance was a different kettle of fish. It was laid down that no field guns could be attached to any corps unless accompanied by a detachment of Regular artillerymen to fight and protect the pieces. Obviously this seriously limited the possibilities for volunteers wishing to train in the management of field guns; yet, paradoxically, the Army was so short of trained personnel that many of the coastal batteries were seriously undermanned, and technically of doubtful value against a determined enemy with the means of assault. As so often was the case in our history volunteer enthusiasm overcame official scruples. There were many cases of local volunteers offering to help man the guns and thereby solving a problem and getting valuable training at the same time. The formation of the Pendennis Artillery Volunteers, for instance, was the direct outcome of enterprising action of this kind. Following a small French landing in the vicinity of Pendennis Castle, which commanded the town and harbour of Falmouth, the inhabitants were seriously concerned about the defences of the Castle, which, with its seventy guns, was held by a single company of forty "invalids" (pensioned-off soldiers). Volunteers offered to help in serving the guns and were taught the drills and procedure by the few gunners available. Eventually the Pendennis Artillery Volunteers not only provided sufficient men to operate all the guns of this fortress, but were able to undertake similar defensive activities in other parts of South-West England.

As in previous wars with France the Government found it necessary to guard against an enemy attack on Ireland, which might be termed the soft underbelly of the United Kingdom. The large Roman Catholic influence made Ireland a hotbed of sedition and late in 1798 an insurrection in that country forced the Government to send Regular troops there, a step which seriously strained the defences of the whole nation. Fortunately the recruitment of volunteers had proceeded apace and there were many instances of self-sacrifice and enterprise on the part of various corps and patriotic individuals. The Honourable Artillery Company, with a gift of £1,000, were among the many units who contributed hadsomely to the financial needs of defence. There were many instances also of officers and men foregoing their rights to pay on active service, and there was no dearth of offers to serve in place of regular troops sent to Ireland.

Naturally the defence of the capital itself loomed large in the general preparations, and the Lord Mayor called a general meeting of all the wards of the City, which issued a joint appeal to all citizens to take arms or at least become special constables "for the duration".

The King's birthday, June 4th 1797, was marked by a grand muster of London's volunteers in Hyde Park in the presence of

King George III himself, attended by the Prince of Wales and the Royal Dukes. A salute of twenty-one guns was fired by the H.A.C. and that Company led in the march past, commanded by Earl Harrington. The Duke of York, brother of the King and C. in C. of the British Army, issued a General Order expressing the King's gratitude and appreciation of the general appearance and martial behaviour of the parade. The number of men in the parade was 8,000, representing sixty-five London corps, and this total was about ten per cent. of the country's volunteer forces at that time. By the end of 1800 the figure had increased in the space of two years to a grand total of nearly 120,000 men, of whom some 24,000 were yeomanry, with a comparatively small number of artillerymen.

This was surely a time of triumph for Britain's volunteer soldiers. They had proved their patriotism on many occasions of crisis, and their enthusiasm had survived many disappointments and rebuffs as Government support and interest waxed and waned with the onset and ending of emergencies.

10

T HE birth of the 19th century indeed marked a peak in the fortunes of the volunteers of Hanoverian times. While all these feverish preparations were being made on the home front the repeated success of Britain's naval forces had been gradually reducing the prospects for a successful outcome to Napoleon's plans for an invasion of England, and in 1801 the state of emergency, in official eyes at least, was ended by the Peace of Amiens. It was to prove an uneasy and transient peace, but no sooner had the Treaty been ratified than the volunteer forces were again disbanded, with the exception of the Yeomanry and the Volunteer Cavalry. This unprecedented decision to retain even a proportion of volunteers in service during peace met with great criticism in Parliament. But the measure for keeping the horsemen was passed, and it rapidly became evident that the Government would have done well to have retained the infantry also. For in less than a year Britain was again at war with France. The bogey of a Napoleonic invasion had re-appeared, and all the old enthusiasm, so dampened by Government parsimony and indifference, flared again more powerfully than ever before. Once more there was the familiar pattern of Government recruitment by statute and independent efforts by patriotic individuals. The first aim of the Government was to create a reserve which would be available for service anywhere in the country; and an Act was rushed through Parliament providing for a ballot to select 50,000 men to serve four years, but exempting all men serving in Yeomanry or Volunteer Corps. A month later the Military

84

Service Act was passed, extending very widely the scope of the previous Act, and intended to rope in anyone who might be of use in repelling or frustrating the enemy.

As a result of all these efforts, there was probably no period in British history that produced more enthusiasm, more energy and more manpower than in this year of crisis, 1803. At the peak of recruitment there were no fewer than 460,300 men under arms or ready to take arms, this total being made up of militia, yeomanry and volunteers, in which all sections of the community were represented. H.R.H. the Duke of Clarence was a private in the Teddington (Middlesex) corps. Pitt the Younger, a great enthusiast for the volunteer movement who was then Warden of the Cinque Ports, raised 3,000 men in that area to help in defence of the Kent and Sussex coasts, and also had much to do with the institution of the Coastal Fencibles, forerunners of the Royal Naval Volunteer Reserve. All over the country factories and warehouses were used for the accommodation of men and horses. The general enthusiasm blurred to the point of oblivion the demarcation lines of class and property, since men of all classes were equally ready to give their services, and inevitably were thrown together. The Elder Brethren of Trinity House founded their own unit and were not more keen than the clerks of the City counting houses. The barristers of the Inns of Court joined together and earned a Royal appellation which stuck. Lord Erskine, the Attorney-General, who led them, was asked by the King at a review who they were: "They're all lawyers, Sir," replied the proud commander. "What!" said His Majesty, "all lawyers? Call them "The Devil's Own!" And so indeed they were from that time forth.

In the midst of the general enthusiasm there were not wanting those who viewed the whole exercise with cynicism and doubted whether the necessary disturbance to public life and commerce and industry would be justified by the military advantages produced. Sir James Macintosh, for example, went on record as saying in the Commons that the volunteer system was "an unfortunate contrivance for taking the maximum of pacific industry for a minimum of military strength". It was calculated, he added, "to call into service the most wealthy, respectable and unwarlike classes and leave unemployed the idle, the profligate, the needy and the robust". He declared London had produced an inversion of the proper order of Society, with lawyers, physicians, merchants and manufacturers serving as private soldiers while hackney coachmen and porters pursued their ordinary occupations.

This was no doubt exaggeration. It was perhaps inevitable that in the capital and other big cities there would be more enthusiasm among the commercial and professional classes than among the crossing sweepers and cabbies. But in the country at large there seemed to be in every breast, whether covered by fustian or broadcloth, a sense of duty and a desire to serve. Well might Pitt say, at the conclusion of this great exercise, that England had "saved herself by her exertions and the rest of Europe by her example".

There might have been some basis for the suggestion that some of the lower classes of Londoners were less ready than the middle and upper classes to give their energy and time to the business of learning to be soldiers. London, after all, had changed a great deal from the London of Tudor times when the apprentices were ever ready for a bit of excitement, lawful or unlawful, and the trained bands would muster at the beat of a drum. But in the smaller towns and cities outside the metropolis the general enthusiasm was unmistakeable. In Edinburgh 4,000 volunteers were enrolled almost overnight and the enthusiasm survived a government cut in allowances. "I wish to remind you," the Colonel of the 2nd Volunteer Battalion Royal Scots told his men, "that we didn't take up arms to please any Minister or set of Ministers, but to defend our country from foreign and domestic enemies." Lord Cockburn in his *Memoirs* gave this picture of a typical Edinburgh volunteer unit:

"Mine was the left flank company of the Western Battalion of Midlothian volunteers. We drilled our two companies almost every night during the four winter months of 1804-5, by torchlight in the ground flat of the George Street Assembly Rooms, which was then all one earthen-floored apartment. This was in addition to our day proceedings on Heriot's Green, or Bruntsfield Links, or with the collected regiment. We became a military population. Any able-bodied man who was not a volunteer or a local militiaman had to explain or apologise for his singularity."

Perhaps it was scenes of this kind that Sir Walter Scott had in mind when he wrote in *The Antiquary* of Jonathan Oldbuck being nonplussed by finding all his men of business thinking more about volunteering than their daily affairs. The following extract, indeed, gives a combined picture of the enthusiasm for volunteering that permeated all classes; of the solicitude of the fair sex for the exertions of their menfolk in the arduous training involved; of the generosity of well-to-do patrons; and of the good-natured contempt with which crusty old bachelors like *The Antiquary* viewed their activities.

Sir Arthur Wardour, it might be remembered, had ventured in conversation with Jonathan Oldbuck to express pleasure at hearing that "our people are getting under arms".

"Under arms," exploded Jonathan. "Lord love thee! Didst thou ever read the History of Sister Margaret? Dost thou remember the nurse's dream in that exquisite work, which she recounts in such agony to Hubble Bubble—when she would have taken up a piece of broadcloth in her vision, lo! it exploded like a great iron cannon; when she put out her hand to save a pirm (reel) it perked up in her face in the form of a pistol.

"My own vision in Edinburgh has been something similar. I called to consult my lawyer; he was clothed in a dragoon's dress, belted and casqued, and about to mount a charger which his writing clerk (habited as a sharpshooter) walked to and fro before his door. I went to scold my agent for having sent me to advise with a madman; he had stuck in his head a plume, which in more sober days he wielded between his fingers, and figured as an artillery officer. My mercer had his spontoon (half-pike) in his hand, as if he measured his cloth by that implement instead of a legitimate yard. The bankers' clerk, who was directed to sum my cash account, blundered it three times, being disordered by the recollection of his military *tellings-off* at the morning drill. I was ill, and sent for a surgeon.

> He came, but valour so had fired his eye,
> And such a falchion glittered on his thigh;

That, by the gods, with such a load of steel
I thought he came to murder, not to heal.

"I had recourse to a physician, but he also was practising a more wholesale mode of slaughter than that which his profession had been supposed at all times to open to him. I hate a gun . . . I detest a drum . . . and they thunder and rattle out yonder on the town's common, so that every volley and roll goes to my heart."

"Dear brother," interjected Miss Griselda Oldbuck, "dinna speak that gate o' the gentlemen volunteers—I am sure they have a most becoming uniform. Weel I wot they have been wet through to the skin twice last week. I met them marching in terrible droukit (drenched) and many a sair hoast (cough) was amang them. And the trouble they take—I am sure it claims our gratitude."

"And I am sure," put in Miss McIntyre, "that my uncle sent twenty guineas to help out their equipment."

"It was to buy liquorice and sugar candy," retorted the cynical donor, "to encourage the trade of the place and to refresh the throats of the officers who had bawled themselves hoarse in the service of their country."

The extent of the national solidity and fervour was clear not only from the tremendous response by volunteers, of whom close on half a million were under arms at the height of the crisis; but also in the attitude of the general public. One striking feature of this particular volunteer movement was that it seemed to bring all classes into close co-operation. The lords of the manor still tended to be in command for military purposes, but they and also the civic leaders of the day recognised the democratic nature of the enterprise, and forged a bond between themselves and men of lesser consequence, realising that this was a national effort which demanded the putting aside of social conventions and notions of precedence.

There are two other passages in *The Antiquary* in which Scott, either consciously or unconsciously, emphasises in one case the democratic and in the other the feudal idea. When Baillie Little-john of Fairport and his fellow magistrates are asked what can be done to billet men and horses of the yeomanry answering the invasion alarm, he says: "Let us take the horses into our ware-houses and the men into our parlours—share our supper with the one and our forage with the other. We have made ourselves wealthy under a free and paternal government, and now is the time to show we know its value."

Later in the same chapter Scott paints the feudal picture: "At length the bugles of the Glenallan yeomanry were heard and the Earl himself . . . appeared at their head in uniform. They made a very handsome, well-mounted squadron, formed entirely out of the Earl's lowland tenants, and were followed by a regiment of 500 men, completely equipped in the Highland dress, whom he had brought down from the Highland glens."

It may not generally be known that in his somewhat fanciful description of the invasion alarm at Fairport Sir Walter Scott was drawing on a personal experience of an actual false invasion alarm which set the Border counties into feverish activity on the night February 2nd, 1804. The circumstances should be recounted as an illustration not only of the vast preparations made throughout the country on a volunteer basis, but also of the speed and enthusiasm with which those concerned reacted to the alarm. In his note on this incident Scott recalled that almost every individual was enrolled either in a military or a civil capacity to resist the long suspended threats of invasion. Beacons were erected all along the coast, and all through the country, to give the signal for everyone to repair to his post, and men "of every description fit to serve" held themselves in readiness at the shortest notice. On the evening in question the man who kept watch on the commanding station at Home Castle, being deceived by some accidental fire in the county of Northumberland, which he took for the corresponding light signal in that county with which his post was in communication, lighted up his own beacon. This signal, coming from the command post, was immediately repeated throughout all the valleys on the English Border. If the beacon at St. Abb's Head had been fired the alarm would have run northward along the coast and roused all Scotland. Fortunately the watch at this important point had the good sense to realise that if there had been a threat of descent on the east coast of England the alarm would have come along the coast and not from the interior of the country. But through the Border counties the alarm spread rapidly and on no occasion was the summons to arms more readily obeyed. In Berwickshire, Roxburghshire and Selkirkshire the volunteers and militia got under arms with a rapidity and alacrity which, considering the distance individuals lived from each other, was surprising. They poured to the alarm-posts on the seacoast in a state so well armed and so completely appointed, with baggage, provisions, etc., as was accounted by the best military judges to render them fit for instant and effectual service.

"There were some particulars in the general alarm," continues Scott, "which are curious and interesting. The men of Liddesdale, the most remote point to the westward which the alarm reached, were so afraid of being late in the field that they put in requisition all the horses they could find; and, when they had thus made a forced march out of their own country, they turned the borrowed steeds loose to find their way back through the hills, and they all got back safe to their own stables. Another remarkable circumstance was the general cry of the inhabitants of the smaller towns for arms, that they might go along with their companions. The Selkirkshire Yeomanry made a remarkable march, for although some of the individuals lived at 20 to 30 miles from the place where they mustered, they were nevertheless embodied so quickly that they were at Dalkeith, their alarm-post, about 1 o'clock on the day succeeding the alarm, with men and horses in good order, although the roads were in a bad state and many of the troopers must have ridden 40 to 50 miles without drawing bridle. Two members of this corps chanced to be absent in Edinburgh on private business. The wife of one of these gentlemen, and the widowed mother of the other, sent the arms, uniforms and chargers to the muster point, that they might join their companions at Dalkeith. The author was very much struck by the answer made to him by the last-mentioned lady, when he paid her some compliments on the readiness which she showed in equipping her son with the means of meeting danger, when she might have left him a fair excuse for remaining absent. 'Sir' she replied with the spirit of a Roman matron, 'none can know better than you that my son is the only prop by which, since his father's death, our family is supported. But I would rather see him dead on that hearth, than hear that he had been a horse's length behind his companions in the defence of his king and country'. The author mentions what was immediately under his own eye, and within his own knowledge;

but the spirit was universal, wherever the alarm reached, both in Scotland and England. The activity which followed on this false alarm was hailed by the country as a propitious omen, that the national force, to which much must naturally have been trusted, had the spirit to look in the face the danger which they had taken arms to repel; and everyone was convinced, that on whichever side God might bestow the victory, the invaders would meet with the most determined opposition from the children of the soil."

The need for the preparations in 1803 was real, since it was clear that Napoleon was indeed planning a full-scale assault on these islands. In May 1804 the Emperor went in person to Boulogne to inspect the preparations for the grand attempt. "Let us be masters of the Channel for six hours," he told Admiral Treville, "and we are masters of the world." At this time the build-up of French forces at Boulogne, planned to reach a total of about 150,000 men, was nearly complete, and the attack was timed to be launched in August. In Britain 300,000 volunteers and militia were under arms, the outcome of frenzied recruiting for the previous twelve months. What, it may be asked, would have happened if the French transports had sailed in August and Napoleon's war-hardened and well-trained troops had landed on British shores? There can be no answer to that question. Napoleon might have been able to provide a stern answer if he had been allowed to stick to his original plan. But Fate took a hand in the game. The French "D-Day" had to be put off for a month because preparations were not completed to the original schedule. And before the end of that month Admiral Treville, the architect and leader of the project, died, leaving his Royal master in a hopeless situation. To go on with the invasion immediately with another commander was impossible. Any further short postponement was impracticable because of the imminent break-up of the weather with the approach of the autumn gales. So the invasion was put off till the spring of 1805. And in the interim a great deal happened to alter the situation. The Allies' pressure on Napoleon elsewhere compelled him to remove his invasion army from Boulogne to Italy. And the six hours' control of the Channel which he had asked for in May was never to be enjoyed. The sea was now commanded by the British Navy and when the various successful manœuvres of Napoleon ended in the decisive victory of Trafalgar on October 21st, 1805, the hopes of conquest were killed, never to be revived.

Napoleon had dreamed of conquest and Britain had had a nightmare of apprehension. But both dream and nightmare passed away, and inevitably the threatened people relapsed into a state of false security. As in the past the end of the emergency was followed by waning official interest in the volunteers. New political influences and thoughts were at work, and the death of Pitt the Younger in January 1806 removed possibly the last defence against the prevailing trend towards economy in military affairs. He had done his utmost to preserve something for which he had fought so much. But in the new atmosphere of 1806, with the thoughts of men turned once more to peaceful pursuits and the thoughts of Parliamentarians towards retrenchment in non-productive fields, War Secretary William Windham had general support for his proposals to reduce the volunteers almost to the point of extinction. He had long taken the attitude that the force had swollen to an uncontrollable extent, and the relief from the threat of invasion brought him the general support of the Government.

The small size of the regular forces of the Crown, which Clode put at 8,000 after the Union with Scotland, meant that in Stuart days the national policy had been that the people would readily defend themselves against a danger and would just as readily return to civilian life when the danger had passed. This pattern is to be observed all through the 17th, 18th and 19th centuries, but during the Napoleonic crisis an Act had been passed, providing for a levy *en masse*, and enacting that men who joined the Volunteers should be exempt from service in the Regular Army or the Militia.

This, as we have seen, helped to bring about the tremendous increase in the Volunteer Force, and Windham, in a Commons debate in 1803, had not minced matters in condemning the whole structure of military power. The Government, he declared, so far from providing an army, had "made it impossible that an army could be provided", because the volunteer system had "locked up" 400,000 of the active population of the country. The actual total of volunteers on December 9th of that year was 463,001, including 82,941 in Ireland.

Pitt naturally took the opposite view, as one might expect of the Warden of the Cinque Ports who had done so much to organise volunteer defences in the most vulnerable area of the British Isles. His opinion was "that to a Regular Army alone, however superior, however excellent, even aided by the militia, we ought not solely to trust; but that in a crisis so full of danger we ought to superadd to the Regular Army some permanent system of National Defence . . . by which the Volunteer Forces of the country, although in a military view inferior to a Regular Army, would, fighting on their own soil for everything dear to individuals and important to a State, be invincible."

That was 1803, and during the time of danger the volunteers stood to in their massive strength. But in 1806 Windham was able to prosecute his antipathy to the volunteer movement in a climate very favourable to his views and aims. Any move which led to a retrenchment in military spending was bound to be popular, and Windham was able to marshal some impressive facts and figures. He maintained in the Commons that in the three and a half years since the stand-to the volunteer system had cost £5,000,000 in allowances. The figure was subsequently shown to be only about three and a half millions, but Windham added to his estimate the expenses undertaken by the volunteers themselves and concluded with some exaggeration that the security which the country had derived from the volunteers had been purchased at "the enormous expense" of 10 millions, "besides depriving our more efficient forces of many men who would otherwise have entered them".

Apart from a natural desire to reduce the Army estimates where they could be reduced without impairing the regular forces of the Crown there was in Windham's heart no sympathy with the volunteer movement. He looked upon it as a body which by its nature could not equal the performances of regular troops, yet at the same time deprived the regular army of worthwhile man-power. He had no objection to men of good family "playing soldiers" as yeomanry or volunteer riflemen, but wanted to stop artisans and labourers from gaining exemption from the militia by joining volunteer units.

"My wish," he said, "is that the Volunteer Corps should consist of such men as it would not be proper to mix with soldiers of the Line, and whom one would not wish to see serving in the conditions of a common soldier; but that the great body of the peasantry—that description of men from whom the Regular Army ought to be recruited—should not be shut up in these Volunteer Corps. Could I see the great mass of the population so far trained as to be able to act either as armed peasantry or to recoup immediately whatever losses the Regular Army might receive in action; then, indeed, I should consider the country invincible."

Sure of Governmental support for his actions, Windham proposed in furtherance of his objects to withdraw allowances, cease the seconding of adjutants and sergeants from the Regular Army, and reduce training periods by two-thirds, thus effecting an estimated annual saving of £878,000. By increasing the personal cost of becoming or remaining a volunteer he hoped to strengthen the militia as an Army reserve and even to stimulate recruiting to the regulars. Nothing, it was laid down, would exempt any otherwise eligible man from militia training except becoming a volunteer at his own expense. He would in that case be paying for the privilege of training as a volunteer.

In fact Windham himself was never able to put this proposal into effect, because the death of Prime Minister Fox in September 1806 meant a change of Government and the end of Windham's short tenure of the War Office. But in the following April Lord Castlereagh introduced a measure which became law as the Local Militia Act; having a very similar purpose and achieving much the same effect.

The new Act created a Local Militia of 60,000 men, which was to be increased in proportion as the Volunteer Force diminished and to supersede the volunteers altogether in time of peace. The original establishment was very quickly exceeded and a year after the passing of the Act 250 regiments of local militia, totalling nearly 200,000 men, were in existence. In another three years the aim of the Government had been more or less achieved, for whereas there were 214,418 local militia, almost equal to the laid-down establishment of 240,388, there were only 68,643 in the volunteer units as compared with an establishment of 99,368. In little more than six years the volunteers had been reduced by seventy-five per cent. In 1803 the volunteer movement had been at the apex of power and popularity. In 1812 it was approaching its nadir. Once again there was eagerness on the part of the Government to dispense as soon as possible with services so gladly given in time of war and so indifferently regarded in peace. The abdication of Napoleon and the Treaty of Paris on May 30th, 1814, had brought peace once more to Europe, to be broken for only a while (although no one knew at the time) by the escape of Napoleon from Elba. But already in 1814, on July 6th, the volunteers had met their Waterloo in the shape of an Order in Council for their disbandment, of course with the thanks of King and Parliament for their loyal services. Getting rid of the volunteers was a simple matter. Standing down the militia was a longer and more intricate business. The Local Militia had been established by Act of Parliament and another Act was required to disembody this great force. The Bill to suspend the ballot was duly passed on May 21st, 1816, and Britain, sleeping blissfully in the arms of Peace and working feverishly in the industrial revolution, forgot about part-time soldiering for two generations.

11

FOR forty years after the final victory over Napoleon the great majority of the inhabitants of Great Britain had no reason to be aware of the existence of part-time forces of any kind. Nevertheless there were units which, for various reasons and usually by their own efforts, had escaped total extinction; and there were occasions of domestic crisis when the Government of the day had cause to be grateful for their existence. It should also be remembered that, although the volunteers and the militia had been officially disembodied, this general stand-down had not applied to the Yeomanry. Indeed, there had always been something special and individual about the Yeomanry, which was a comparatively modern development of the volunteer movement, but, once established, had a continuous, if sometimes tenuous, existence till it was merged with other movements in the Territorial Force in 1907. One reason for this continuity was the horse. Farmers and landowners, anyone indeed who owned or had access to horses, were always assured of mounts; and there was a degree of companionship, based on identical local interests, which helped in the preservation of units of volunteer cavalry. Riding to hounds or riding to an exercise were not basically very different.

The other reason was the value of the horse in military activities. The advantages of having a number of horsemen readily available to move rapidly to a scene of action were exploited by civic and county authorities and by the Crown on many occasions from 1761, when the first Yeomanry Corps came into existence. During

Above, the London Military Foot Association putting down the Gordon Riots, 1780; *below*, George III reviews the Light Horse Volunteers of London and Westminster on Wimbledon Common 1798

Above, Queen Victoria opening the inaugural meeting of the National Rifle Association, from which a great number of volunteers were drawn; *below*, The Hyde Park Review of Volunteers, 1860

the next thirty years the yeomanry had its ups and downs in common with the volunteer movement, but in 1794 more than 5,000 part-time cavalry were rapidly enlisted. Soon afterwards the Provisional Cavalry Act created what might be called the equestrian equivalent of the Militia. It required every owner of ten horses to provide and equip one horseman; and less affluent inhabitants had to combine in furnishing horsemen at the rate of one for every ten horses owned. This Act was not popular with the rural communities and an amending Act was passed allowing the counties to substitute Yeomanry for Provisional Cavalry in their quotas. This move stimulated recruiting so much that although the Provisional Cavalry were embraced in the general stand-down after the Peace of Amiens the Yeomanry units were allowed to remain in being. This circumstance permitted a rapid mustering of volunteer horsemen in the crisis of 1803, and by December of that year more than 40,000 Yeomanry were ready for service.

The outbreak of the Reform Bill riots in 1830 necessitated a call on the Yeomanry units but there was also a hurried re-establishment of volunteer foot units in various big cities, for use in maintaining public order. It was only in the previous year that Sir Robert Peel's Metropolitan Police Act had brought into being a police force for London—the Peelers—and not for some years afterwards were similar bodies established in the provinces. In any case, although the "Bobby" represented a big advance on the constables and watchmen appointed by the parish, who had hitherto been the only representatives of law and order, he was still scarcely fitted, nor intended, for the suppression of mob violence or insurrection. This, in those days, could only be done by a show of arms, and the use of them if need be. Obviously the employment of regular troops for these purposes wasted both time and money, and in 1830 the Government, not for the first nor the last time, had recourse to local Yeomanry regiments and resuscitated Volunteer units.

For this reason, of the 20,000 volunteers officially enlisted as being embodied in 1832 the great proportion consisted of Yeomanry. During the next decade little was heard of the activities of these units, but as the middle of the century drew near the country was torn by domestic strife and apprehensive of political and military moves on the Continent. There were many old soldiers who felt that Britain's defences were dangerously inadequate, and at their head was the Duke of Wellington, now nearly eighty. In 1848 the Duke, who two years before had retired from politics but remained Commander-in-Chief of the British Army, organised the London military defences against the Chartist rioters; and this trouble, as well as the abdication of Louis Philippe, the proclamation of the French Republic and revolutionary activities in other parts of the Continent, aroused grave doubts in his mind. These he expressed in a famous letter to General Sir John Burgoyne, who had been commanding engineer on Wellington's staff and had just been appointed Inspector-General of Fortifications.

The country was so defenceless, declared the aged Duke, that if the fleet failed to prevent an enemy landing on British shores, whatever opposition could be mustered in such an emergency "could not prevail against the fire of musketry and cannon and the sabres and bayonets of disciplined troops". He had tried in vain, he said, to awaken the Government to a sense of the danger. This warning, made by a man revered for his skill as a general and his sagacity as a politician, naturally caused disquiet in intelligent circles but left the Government apparently indifferent. In the next few years other warnings also went unheeded until, in 1852, Sir Charles Napier addressed a letter to the Commons advocating a scheme for ensuring the defence of Britain, during the absence overseas of regular armed forces, by an efficient establishment of volunteer corps and militia. These recommendations some years later were to form the basis of the new volunteer movement, but at the time they received scant attention from the Government. Nevertheless, at this stage Horace Walpole, afterwards the Earl of Orford, a son of Robert Walpole, the great 18th-century Whig statesman, became Secretary for War and apparently looked with more favour than his predecessors on a number of units which had contrived by various means to keep alive after the stand-down of 1814. The means usually adopted was the conversion of the volunteer unit into a rifle club, and these clubs were tolerated because there was nothing authority could complain of in men coming together at their own expense to practise the art of shooting. One of these units had a particularly interesting history, starting with the formation in 1803 of the Duke of Cumberland's Sharpshooters. The corps survived the 1814 stand-down and carried on unofficial activities as a rifle club until 1835, when the Duchess of Kent granted it the title of Royal Victoria Rifles in honour of a Princess who, very shortly afterwards, was to begin her long and glorious reign as Queen of England. For a number of years the corps carried on a semi-official existence, but the many efforts of its commander, Captain Hans Busk, to gain for his unit official recognition and permission to operate as a proper military unit failed until towards the end of 1852.

For some years a number of prominent citizens of Exeter had been endeavouring to obtain Government permission to form themselves into a rifle company, but with no success until 1852, when Walpole agreed. Queen Victoria signed the commissions for the formation of the South Devon Volunteer Rifle Association, and so the men of Exeter constituted the first regiment to be commissioned in the new volunteer movement. A breach had been made and was followed by others. Captain Hans Busk renewed his application, and the Royal Victoria Rifles were given authority to form a battalion of four companies of seventy-five men each.

These and subsequent commissions were signed under the Volunteer Act of 1804, and in no way represented any decision by the Government to favour a general revival of the movement. This was made clear when Mr. Nathaniel Bousfield of Liverpool tried unsuccessfully to get permission to raise a corps of riflemen in that city. After four years more of agitation this persevering personality had still had only rebuffs for his pains, and not until 1859, when the sabre-rattling of Napoleon III caused new unrest in Europe, was the Liverpool Volunteer Corps commissioned. In the meantime the Crimean war of 1854–5 and the Indian Mutiny of 1857 had drawn public attention once more to the inadequacy of Britain's home defences in the absence of regular troops abroad. It was not even possible to bring our troops in India up to the required strength without seriously depleting the garrisons at home, and it seemed that the advocates of a revival of volunteer and militia forces had common sense on their side. Yet even in the face of these facts there was opposition in authoritative quarters, a situation which seems incredible having regard to the history of previous volunteer movements in time of crisis. The newspapers, both by leading articles and in their correspondence columns, were virtually unanimous in advocating the formation of a new volunteer army, and *The Times* urged the Government to adopt the idea as "both reasonable and opportune". But the new G.O.C.-in-C. of the Army, H.R.H. the Duke of Cambridge, was most emphatic in opposition.

"These (volunteer corps) will never answer; they are unmanageable bodies and would ruin our Army." Thus the Duke wrote to Lord Panmure, Secretary of State for War. A little later we find the Duke being so illogical as to express the opinion that recruiting for the Regular Army was not sufficient for the demand, yet still pour cold water on the idea of a volunteer corps.

"I dismiss at once from my mind," he declared in another letter to Lord Panmure, "all the ideas in the public prints about volunteer corps. If such a system were to be adopted, the spirit of the Regular Army would be destroyed and jealousies would at once be engendered. Volunteers would do as much or as little duty as they liked, and in fact they would be an armed and very dangerous rabble. Some gentlemen are coming forward promising to raise 1,000 men for a Lt.-Colonelcy; others 100 for an Ensigncy, but none has as yet found anything like that number of men, and I doubt much whether any will succeed in their expectations." So vehement was the Duke in this matter, and so uncompromising his dislike of volunteers, that the only alternative he proposed to preserve the defences of the country was to form a Foreign Legion! With thousands of men, young and middle-aged and old, willing and eager to carry out onerous duties in the interests of their country, the head of the Army could visualise only a body of mercenaries. At this time, unfortunately, Lord

Panmure supported the Duke's attitude. But the march of events was too strong for both. By January 1859 relations with France had worsened to such an extent that even the Government was stirred from lethargy and compelled to take notice of the popular demand for military readiness and preparation. Various factors combined to force the official hand. Public clamour for a resumption of volunteer soldiering was supported by the fact that the Lords-Lieutenant of many counties had already acted by forming various corps against the time when their actions should receive official encouragement and support. The situation was certainly peculiar. Although the volunteer movement had been in abeyance for many years the Lords-Lieutenant had retained their powers over any local forces which might be recruited. But unless and until there was an Order in Council empowering them to form such bodies, any action of the kind lacked the force of law.

In the meantime the efforts of many far-seeing and responsible men were bent to the task of breaking down official opposition. Mr. Bousfield, Captain Busk and Sir Duncan McDougall were active in various parts of the country. There was a public meeting in Bristol addressed by several eminent West Country gentlemen, and a big meeting at St. Martin's Hall, London—on April 16th, 1859—"to consider the weakness of our national defences". There was general Public and Press support for these and other efforts; and *The Times*, subscribing to the widely-held opinion that standing armies and fleets were not sufficient to defend the country, declared:

"A mere artificial organisation which may be demolished by a campaign, a pestilence or a tempest does not give a fit security to the people, who may at any moment be deprived of its services. There can only be one true defence of a nation like ours—a large and permanent Volunteer Force, supported by the spirit and patriotism of our younger men, and gradually indoctrinating the country with military knowledge. We are the only people in the world who do not have such a force. We want men of ordinary occupation, trained by a certain amount of skill, to support the regular force either in the field or in the fortress."

Mr. Bousfield had by this time raised an unofficial body of

Liverpool volunteers, and it was on his behalf and in general support of the incipient volunteer movement that Sir Duncan McDougall wrote to the Secretary for War, then General Jonathan Peel, on April 28th, pleading for a change in the Government's views. This and other expressions of popular favour helped towards the desired end, and *The Times* continued to lend powerful support. On May 9th that newspaper published a forceful poem, "Riflemen Form", which Lord Tennyson, the Poet Laureate, afterwards admitted to have been written by him, and three days later a War Office Circular was sent by General Peel to the Lords-Lieutenant authorising the raising of a volunteer corps under the Act of 1804. This was followed by a Supplementary Circular (said to have been inspired by the Prince Consort).

On May 13th, Lord Rosslyn wrote from the War Office to Sir Duncan McDougall: "I am directed by the Secretary for War to acknowledge receipt of your letter and to acquaint you that a circular has been issued from this Department, informing the Lords-Lieutenant of the Counties of the conditions on which Her Majesty's Government will recommend to Her Majesty the adoption of the services of volunteer corps in their respective counties."

Sir Duncan, overjoyed, sent this letter on to Mr. Bousfield and told him: "I believe you and the other gentlemen comprising your corps may consider that your patriotism has been greatly the means of inducing the Government to issue the circular. I hope the expectations I expressed to the War Minister regarding the probable strength and efficiency of your corps may be fully realised."

Thus ended seven years of disappointment and frustration for Mr. Bousfield. On June 11th he received the first commission granted to a volunteer under the new scheme; and on June 15th he marched at the head of 180 men, armed, equipped and showing military precision and bearing, to the Liverpool Exchange, where his band played the National Anthem and a civic reception was given the new corps.

Although at this early stage the War Office conceived an organisation on the general lines of that of 1804, there was one important difference. Members of the new corps to be raised had to undertake to provide their own arms and equipment and defray all expenses of themselves and their unit, except in the event of being assembled for actual service. This provision was obviously designed to restrict service in the volunteers to those able to pay for the privilege of serving their country, and to ensure that other men would serve either in the Militia or the Regular Army. In 1804 the Volunteer Force was regarded as not only a defence force but also a reservoir of manpower for the regular army. In 1859 it was deemed in official quarters to be an individual force having nothing to do with either the Militia or the Regular Army. From that time forth, indeed, the volunteers were volunteers in their own right, independent of other bodies. No longer a collection of local defence units, but a Corps with national commitments, bound by these conditions to serve in any part of the Kingdom to which they might be called by the exigencies of war.

In February 1859 two months before the issue of the War Office circular, "unofficial" enrolment of volunteers had reached more than 60,000. By the end of May, after three weeks of official recruiting, the total had swollen to 134,000. A British volunteer movement was once more in full swing, and this time it had come to stay.

The Government now began to take the movement very seriously, by attempting to obtain uniformity in dress and arms and so identifying it much more closely with the Regular Army. From the start it had been emphasised that arms, although supplied at the expense of individual volunteers or their patrons, should be subject to War Office regulations to secure uniformity of calibre. In July of the same year the Government decided to issue Enfield rifles at Government expense at the rate of twenty-five to every 100 men, with a proviso that there would be a 100 per cent issue for any corps going on active service. Arrangements were made for representatives of companies to attend courses of instruction at the Army School of Musketry, at Hythe, with the intention that they should return to their units fully capable of passing on the instruction. The matter of a general uniform was less easily settled, touching as it did on individual tastes and feelings and the local traditions of the various companies. The dark-blue tunics and trousers so much favoured were frowned on by authority as providing too good a target for the enemy. Eventually a uniform of blouse, trousers, greatcoat and cap in light grey was recommended for general adoption, although individual O.C.s were not obliged to abandon distinctive dress if they wished to retain it.

The supplementary circular already referred to was designed to limit service in the Volunteers to those who would not in any circumstances join the Regular Army and for similar reasons had no desire to be enlisted in the Militia. And a system of training was devised which would fit in with the civilian activities of professional and commercial gentlemen and country landowners who, it was expected, would form the great part of the new Force.

The terms of the circular of May 12th also did much to dissipate the opposition of the Duke of Cambridge, who had not welcomed the idea of a volunteer corps fighting alongside regular troops (and possibly, in his view, contaminating them!). But the warm fervour of the men who flocked to sign made him realise that such spirit should be encouraged, so long as it was expressed in terms consistent with his ideas of military discipline and efficiency. The Duke, then a comparatively young man, lived long enough to see volunteers fighting alongside regular troops with great skill, courage and distinction.

It is fair to say that the Duke had had a great deal to do with the drafting of the May 12th circular, because although he disapproved strongly of any idea of using volunteer units to reinforce the regulars in India or anywhere else, he did approve in principle of a volunteer force at home, qualifying his approval by insisting that the efficiency of such a Force must be of a high standard. The Duke had always been actuated by a desire to strengthen the regular forces of the country. They were so far below strength that it was impossible to send the required number of Line troops abroad and have enough at home to man coastal defences and garrison towns. His Royal Highness did not consider that either the militia or such volunteers as existed were capable of taking on such duties; and since the militia was at a very low standard of recruitment and volunteer units few in number and short of training, this was probably the correct view. For this reason the Duke advocated intensifying recruitment for the Regular Army and the Militia, but at the same time agreeing to the raising of volunteer corps in principle, stipulating only that the units thus raised must be under military discipline and use arms and equipment of the same design and calibre as those issued to regular regiments. It will be seen that these general recommendations, made a few months before the War Office circular of May 12th, did indeed form the basis of that circular.

No movement so personal as the Volunteer Force, and with such a patchwork history, could be expected to achieve the Duke's standards overnight or without a great deal of experiment and undergoing many difficulties. Inevitably there were growing pains, problems, errors from haste and inexperience, and an understandably slow appreciation, in the minds of many volunteers and some of their officers, of the magnitude of the "new deal". It was not easy for these men to realise that far greater Government importance was attached to the new Force than to any previous body of the kind. And not everyone took kindly to the fact, which gradually emerged, that the new-style volunteers, instead of endeavouring to imitate in every way the dress, drills and general behaviour of regular troops, were now to develop their own style and methods. If it came to fighting they would be engaged mainly in guerrilla warfare against an enemy already on British soil, and therefore have an independent role as riflemen stalking, rounding up and harassing hostile forces. This novel idea naturally suggested the provision of ancillary services, and soon there had come into existence Pioneer companies composed of men accustomed to labour with pick and shovel, and practised in the arts of hedging and ditching. From this to engineering was but a step, and early in 1860 the 1st Middlesex Volunteer Engineers appeared on the scene. With equal rapidity other arms of the Service were duplicated in the new Volunteer Force, and so speedy and fruitful was the growth that even those who had worked hardest and with most enthusiasm for the revival were astonished at the acceleration. At the opening of Parliament in

January 1860 the speech from the throne described the Volunteers as having added "an important element to our system of national defence". These sentiments were echoed and others expressed in the subsequent Parliamentary debates; and if anything were still required to emphasise the important part now played by the Volunteers, it was provided by a levee held on March 7th at St. James's Palace, where 2,500 volunteer officers were presented to Her Majesty and the Prince Consort. More than 1,000 of those officers dined later at St. James's Hall under the chairmanship of the Duke of Cambridge, who less than three years earlier had written so scornfully and unhelpfully about the volunteer idea. Now he proposed a toast to the success of the volunteer movement, and made the important point that the movement must be continuous and devoted entirely to defence. I also quote another part of the Duke's speech because I consider it confirms my own view that one should not seek too narrow a definition of "Volunteer".

"A great Empire like ours", said H.R.H., "should always be in a position of perfect security. We should be able to say to the world: 'Come, if you dare!' It might be true that we are not a military nation, but I challenge anyone to instance a country where such a display of military spirit can be found. The Militia and the Regular Army—are they not all volunteers? All, whether members of the Regular Army, the Militia or the Volunteers, come from the same source, and are animated by the same feelings in coming forward, each in their respective services, for the defence of the country."

Later that year, on June 23rd, a great review was held in Hyde Park and was eulogistically referred to by Sir Theodore Martin in his *Life of the Prince Consort*. *The Times* carried a report on June 25th describing how Her Majesty was accompanied in an open carriage by the King of the Belgians, Princess Alice and Prince Arthur, with the Prince Consort riding at her side. There were 18,450 volunteers under arms for this review. It was led by the 1st Huntingdonshire Mounted Rifles, who passed the saluting base at 4.30 p.m., and ninety minutes later the 25th Cheshire Company brought up the rear.

"The troops kept the best of time," ran the report. "Had the operation been rehearsed several times instead of the fifty corps never having seen one another till that hour, it could not have been better executed. Of the worth of the demonstration there can be no doubt, for it proved England to be at heart a military nation."

At a dinner the same evening the Prince Consort said: "We have witnessed this day a scene which will never fade from the memory of those who had the good fortune to be present—the representatives of the independence, education and industry of this country in arms, to testify their devotion to their country and their readiness to lay down their lives in its defence. The Volunteer Force already exceeds 130,000 men; to what extent this country is capable of exerting itself in real danger is shown by the number of volunteers in 1804 reaching the extraordinary figure of 479,000. We are apt to forget, however, that in contrast with any other country in the world all our services are composed exclusively of volunteers—the Navy, Coast Guard, Coast Volunteers, Army, Militia, Yeomanry, Constabulary, and Volunteers. May the noble and patriotic spirit which such a fact reveals remain unimpaired!"

A general Order issued after the Review conveyed Her Majesty's "very great satisfaction".

12

THE War Office circular of May 1859 had an immediate response throughout the country. Liverpool, of course, had long been poised for the leap into activity; and Manchester, Birmingham and other big cities were not far behind in acquiring corps. Universities and public schools also quickly formed detachments, and in a very short time the number of volunteers had topped 100,000. General public interest in this new movement was fostered by the Press, and correspondence in the newspapers raged on such subjects as the role of the volunteers in war, how they should be dressed and drilled. The letter in *The Times* of Mr. Henry Drummond, M.P. for West Surrey, may be taken as an example:

"The best uniform for a rifle corps composed chiefly of inhabitants of country towns and villages is a common round frock, such as is worn by labourers, with a brown soft leather belt . . . to hold the cartridges, and a black or green wideawake hat."

Mr. Drummond justified his advocacy of a smock—for that presumably is what he meant—by declaring that if made of unbleached linen it would be "the colour of stubble, decayed fern leaves, sticks, etc.", and almost invisible. Further, it could be worn over or without any underclothing and would have pockets for keeping powder, firing caps and food for the day.

In this letter we see developing the idea of volunteers who would serve in the fields and under the hedgerows of their native countryside in a form of guerrilla warfare against invading forces. The old idea of bright-coloured uniforms with gold facings and brasses that would reflect the sun and stand out against an ordinary landscape was dying, and the conception of military clothing was approaching nearer to the khaki of the South African war. The volunteers of 1803 had looked brave and colourful on parade, but would have been sitting ducks in a field of stubble. The new volunteers might be doomed to a drab existence sartorially but were more likely to become expert in the art of warfare and could count on a better chance of survival.

Some of the advice given to the new volunteers was from doubtful sources, the product of cranks theorising without the benefit of practical experience. Not so the sage advice of Sir Charles Napier, the author seven years before of a famous letter to the Commons. His recommendation to volunteer officers, printed by *The Times* on May 24th, 1859, ran:

"Let each man carry two small cartridge boxes made to slide on a girdle round the waist so that one may be carried before and one behind, thus the weight would be more easily carried.

"Get some old soldier for your adjutant to teach you, not a long course of drill, but just seven things, viz:

1. To face right and left at the word of command.
2. To march in line and column.
3. To extend and close files as light infantry support.
4. To change front in extended and close order.
5. To relieve the skirmishers.
6. To form 'solid squares' and 'rallying squares'.
7. To form an advanced guard.

"These seven things are all you require. Do not let anyone persuade you to learn more.

"Let your practice at a target be constant. Also habituate your corps to long marches of from fifteen to twenty miles, with arms and ammunition, and also to running, or 'double quick time'.

"Do not be exclusive in forming your corps. Take your game-keepers as your comrades and any of your labourers that will enrol themselves. A gentleman will find no braver or better comrades than amongst his own immediate neighbours and tenants. *Should you require to throw up a breastwork, they will be more handy with the spades and pickaxes than yourselves.*"

The italics are mine. To mid-Victorian readers of *The Times* there could have been nothing strange in the gallant General's secondary reason for incorporating gamekeepers and labourers in a volunteer unit.

So much for 19th-century military ideas and class consciousness. Today we have democracy, equality and a bulky Army Manual.

But in spite of Parliamentarians' ideas of smocks for yokels, and militarists' patronising and calculating advice about gamekeepers and labourers, there was a new spirit abroad. The volunteer idea had undergone a metamorphosis during the years in which it had lain dormant. In 1803 there had been a great rush of recruits impelled by many things, including a wish to escape the ballot or a desire to be preserved from the activities of the Naval press gangs. In 1859 these fears no longer existed. The rush to enlist was inspired purely by a will to serve and protect King and country.

The greatest and most powerful movement was made, of course, in London. There was already a nucleus, and the Royal Victoria Rifles were soon able not only to treble the meagre strength they had hitherto been allowed, but also to provide officers for the new corps which were being formed almost daily. There was a great vogue for forming corps restricted to certain professions and vocations. The "Devil's Own" were revived by the lawyers, and companies labelled "Artists", "Civil Service" and "Working Men's College" soon came into existence to show how widespread was the movement. It was about this time that Lord Elcho helped to form "The London Scottish", resigning his seat in Parliament for a year to take the command and get the regiment properly established. The national movement owed much to the individual volunteer, but also a great deal to the unselfish enthusiasm of prominent men in politics, commerce and the professions who gave wholeheartedly of their time and energy, and often dipped deeply into their pockets to ensure that the new movement was established on a firm efficient foundation.

The enthusiasm of the great provincial cities was every whit as warm as that of Londoners. Glasgow and Edinburgh were the centres of recruitment in Scotland, and each in 1859 followed her great traditions. Glasgow, from its position as a great commercial centre, its proximity to the sea and its great shipbuilding industry, had always been aloof from rebellious factions and her citizens and chief magistrates had ever been staunch supporters of law and order. In 1745, under threat from the Young Pretender, a public meeting passed a resolution to raise as many men as could bear arms, and ask for government assistance in the defence of the city. Several volunteer units were formed in Glasgow over the next 100 years, and, like others, passed into inactivity as each successive crisis passed. But there remained the nucleus of a volunteer force ready to take advantage of the events of May 1859 and on May 5th, a week before the issue of the War Office circular, 300 citizens met in Glasgow and formed themselves into a unit. They were said at the time to be representative of the whole of Glasgow in class, trade and district. University students, bankers, lawyers, accountants, grocers, warehousemen—everyone in every walk of life—became infected with the general enthusiasm. A leading Glasgow citizen, Mr. Archibald K. Murray, whose letter to a Glasgow newspaper had brought about the meeting, claimed that the response of Glasgow to the War Office circular was twice that of London. Within a month 3,000 men had signed on and in another three months the total was 10,000.

Eleven years previously gentlemen and farmers of the Western Lowlands had formed themselves into the Lanarkshire Yeomanry, and almost immediately achieved Royal favour and recognition. They formed an escort for Queen Victoria and the Prince Consort on the State visit to Glasgow in 1849 and were afterwards given permission to bear the title of Queen's Own Royal Regiment, Glasgow. Men of this regiment half a century later were to be with the first British troops in South Africa.

Loyalty to the Crown and enthusiasm for the cause has always been expressed by the citizens of Bristol and the county people of the West Country. It was the loyalty of Bristol that rang the death-knell of Monmouth's ill-fated invasion; and in the next 200 years the people of Bristol and Somerset and Gloucestershire answered every call. In 1745 the Mayor of Bristol was the prime mover in the formation of an "Association for the defence of the Town and H.M. Government", with more than 1,000 enlisting; and the farmers and landowners of the Cotswolds formed a troop of Yeomanry. More than 1,300 men rallied to the call for volunteers made by the "Anti-American Committee" of Bristol in 1779, and nearly twenty years later the same readiness to serve against possible danger from France was evinced by the citizens. A medal was struck on that occasion bearing the motto "In Danger Ready", and this was the motto used sixty years later by the 1st Gloucestershire (Bristol) Rifle Volunteers when, following the big public meeting in Bristol already mentioned, this battalion was formed.

Lancashire and the North-west have a history of somewhat divided loyalties. While the men of Bristol were mustering for the King of England in 1743 some volunteer bodies were being raised in Lancashire in the interests of Bonny Prince Charlie. But with the suppression of the rebellion partizanship was forgotten and the thoughts of men turned from supporting factions to the need for preserving the national heritage. Thus in 1782 the formation of a Manchester Military Association and of a similar Association of Liverpool citizens "for their own defence". The records of the volunteers of those times are full of references to the willingness of men to pay for the privilege of being associated with the movement. In 1863 we find John Bolton, a Liverpool merchant, raising and equipping at his own expense ten companies to form the 1st Battn. Royal Liverpool Volunteers; while at Preston they formed a Yeomanry Corps to serve in case of invasion or imminent danger thereof. Each member of the corps agreed to mount, arm, clothe and equip himself at his own expense, to serve without pay and contribute to the cost of training. Another signal instance of Lancashire zeal was the munificent gesture of the Preston Volunteers, raised in 1793, who not only followed the example of many corps in declining pay or allowances of any kind, but also raised by private subscription a large sum as a contribution to the defence of the country.

Thus early in their career the new volunteers were very well equipped, even though largely by their own efforts and the

Above, Members of the London Scottish Volunteer Corps in 1860, soon after their formation; *below*, a trooper of the Warwickshire Yeomanry Cavalry, 1873

Civil Service Rifle Volunteers in camp in 1897; *below*, an artist's impression of the capture of Jacobsdal, the City Imperial Volunteers' baptism of fire during the Boer War

generous support of wealthy sponsors. At a big review of all the volunteers of Lancashire, held in Knowsley Park at the invitation of the Earl of Derby in the autumn of 1860, there were no fewer than four battalions of artillery, one composed entirely of shipyard workers employed by the Cunard Company; and another commanded by a Colonel Brown, said to contribute £3,000 a year to its maintenance.

Another proud commandant at this parade was Colonel Bousfield, at the head of the 1st Lancashire Brigade of infantry, which by now numbered 2,210 men including 320 cadets from Liverpool College. Boys of Rossall School also had a detachment of cadets in another brigade.

Soon afterwards 22,000 men were reviewed by the Queen in Holyrood Park, Edinburgh. At this and other places where reviews took place there was always tremendous enthusiasm and great expressions of loyalty on the part of the troops engaged; and considerable interest evinced by the general public. Of course there were those who poured scorn on the whole idea and others, less objectionable, who affected to regard it with amused tolerance. The cartoonists and satirists of the day aimed their shafts at such convenient targets, as their fraternity have done through the ages. But the volunteers persisted in giving an impression of willingness to make themselves efficient and reliable; and before long the new Force was accepted as something the country badly needed and henceforth could not do without.

A small yet significant indication that the volunteers were now accepted was the issue of a General Order by the Duke of Cambridge about the time of the Edinburgh review, directing all non-commissioned officers and privates of the Regular Army to salute Volunteer officers in uniform, and guards and sentries to present arms when armed bodies of volunteers passed by. This was indeed a gesture from one who, only a short time before, had expressed misgivings about the idea of volunteers being identified in any way with the regular forces. Later that year, when Parliament rose, Her Majesty included in her speech from the throne a reference to the "gratification and pride" with which she had witnessed the rapid progress in military efficiency already made by the Volunteer Force—progress which was "highly honourable to their spirit and patriotism."

The new Volunteers were visualised by the authorities as mainly riflemen, and their secondary role of guerrillas demanded a high standard of skill and accuracy in the use of the rifle. The decision of the Government to issue rifles of a similar pattern to all units, and to put selected volunteer officers through a course of instruction at Hythe, were two important steps in the required direction. Another and even more far-reaching move was the introduction of the competitive element by the formation, in November 1859, of the National Rifle Association. This body, in the foundation of which Lord Elcho played a leading part, had the avowed objects of providing shooting practice for the volunteers and making the rifle as popular with Victorians as the bow had been in earlier times. For the second reason the Association was open to everyone, not only volunteers, and as a result its competitions from the very start were representative of all classes of shooting enthusiasts, as well as attracting many entrants from abroad. This factor had the effect of improving the marksmanship of the volunteers by confronting them with the highest standards of shooting in Britain and the Continent.

Sidney Herbert, Secretary for War, was elected first President of the N.R.A., and the Prince Consort consented to be patron. Queen Victoria gave an annual prize of £250 to be competed for only by volunteers; but there were a number of other prizes, including one given by the Prince Consort, which were open to all comers. The range was of 1,000 yards on Wimbledon Common, and was opened on July 2nd, 1860, by Her Majesty, who, under the guidance of Lord Elcho, pulled a string attached to a rifle carefully adjusted to a target at 400 yards' range, and duly scored a bull's-eye. The first winner of the Queen's Prize was Edward Ross, nineteen years old, of the 7th North York Volunteers, and he also won the Ladies' Prize in competition with some of the best Swiss and German marksmen. There was tremendous public interest in these inaugural competitions—so many people crowded on to the Common to watch the shooting that the meeting realised £2,000 in gate money.

At first the newly-formed volunteers served in separate companies of 100 men each, but this was soon found to be unworkable and eventually, although not without much argument and opposition, the Force was reconstituted into battalions of eight or ten companies, each battalion having seconded to it an adjutant and a field officer of the Regular Army. Another change, which met with no opposition, was a relaxation by the Government of the original stipulation that volunteers should receive no pay except while on active service, and would have to meet the costs of equipment and training. In 1860 the Government decided on a free issue of rifles, and in July 1861 a grant of £133,275 was made. This was for the yeomanry as well as for the volunteers, and as there were now 150,000 riflemen, each of whom cost about £10 to maintain, it was obvious that even with this Government grant the cost of running the Force would still have to be met by private individuals, either the volunteers themselves or well-to-do patrons. But as it became clearer that the volunteers were justifying the optimism of their supporters in the Government, so there came about progressive improvement in their financial circumstances. In this year of 1861 the volunteers actually outnumbered the Regular Army, which then consisted of 146,000 men. Moreover there was plenty of evidence in various parts of the country that thus early in their existence the training and parade demeanour of some volunteer corps would stand comparison with the average standard of regular soldiers. These considerations, together with considerable public interest in the matter, led to a Supply Vote in the Commons in 1862 for an increase of £122,880 in the grant to volunteers—still nowhere near enough to save the men from having to dig into their own pockets, but a step in the right direction. Another welcome move was the appointment of Regular Army drill sergeants to volunteer battalions.

On May 16th of the same year a Royal Commission under the chairmanship of Viscount Eversley and including six representatives of the volunteers, two civilians and three Regular Army men, was appointed to inquire into the condition of the Volunteer Force in Great Britain, and unearthed some interesting facts. It seemed clear from the evidence given that the Force, so far from being formed mostly from the middle classes and privileged sections of the community, was to a great extent manned by working-class individuals. In Scotland as a whole about half the volunteers were artisans but in Glasgow, it was estimated, about seventy-five per cent of the volunteers were working-class citizens, and the same pattern was to be observed in the big cities of England, including London. Evidence of this kind indicated the democratic pattern of the new force, but it also provided a reason for a noticeable falling-off in membership after the initial enthusiasm had waned. In nearly all the corps members had not only to pay entrance fees and annual subscriptions, but were also expected to provide their own uniforms. As time went on uniforms required replenishing, and men began to leave the movement for the simple reason that they could no longer afford to remain members.

On the other hand, evidence given before the Commission showed quite clearly that the movement had helped to improve public behaviour by encouraging into the volunteer companies young men who had formerly idled on streets corners or in public houses, created breaches of the peace or indulged in vandalism. The evidence of John Pettie, an artisan who was a sergeant in the London Scottish, may be cited as an example. He said that the artisans, since becoming volunteers, had improved socially, morally and politically. He added that "a man who is a volunteer is worth 3s. a week more to a jobbing master than one who is not." High praise indeed, in an age when 18s. was a good wage for a labourer. These and other testimonies impressed the Commissioners who duly reported their gratification in being able to state that "the present condition of the volunteer force is, generally speaking, satisfactory, and we believe that, by steady perseverance in the course hitherto pursued, and by due discipline, it will be a valuable auxiliary to the British Army as a means of defence." Naturally the recommendations of the Commissioners were in line with this sentiment. They reported the existence of 162,681 enrolled volunteers (662 light horse, 24,363 artillery, 2,904 engineers, 656 mounted rifles and 134,096 riflemen) and recommended a capitation grant of 20s. for every man satisfying certain conditions as to his general efficiency and drill attendances, with 10s. extra for every volunteer who had carried out a stipulated amount of firing practice. These proposals were ratified by the Government in a Consolidation Act and with other measures and reliefs helped to stay the feared falling-off in recruitment. Indeed, from the end of 1862 there was a progressive increase in the number of "efficients" in the Volunteer Force. Ten years later, coinciding with the introduction of Army reforms which very closely concerned the volunteer movement, the official regard for the Force as an integral part of the armed forces of the Crown was shown in a very marked way. Autumn manœuvres had been organised for the Regular Army in Hampshire, and more than 4,000 volunteers and yeomanry efficients exercised alongside 23,000 regulars for a fortnight.

13

THE Army reforms referred to at the end of the previous chapter were initiated in 1871, but had been preceded by a departmental Committee set up in 1869 to inquire into the state of the Volunteer Force. Various recommendations were made and adopted by the Government, leading to major reforms which under the Army Regulations Act of 1871 integrated the Force still more closely with the Regular Army and confirmed its status as a branch of the armed might of the nation.

For many years the minds of sagacious, liberal and progressive men had been agitated by the general inadequacy of our defences and the maladministration of and corruption in the Regular Army. The Crimean War with its costly mistakes in administration, its poor organisation which cost the lives of so many brave men, and the want of military skill in many of its leading officers, made the country aware of a great number of unpleasant facts. National opinion was still further disturbed by the Indian Mutiny, which occurred a year after the end of the unprofitable war with Russia, and in the following year, 1858, the attempt on the life of Napoleon III in Paris and the subsequent worsening of relations between Britain and France increased public alarm. These events led, as we have already seen, to the great revival of the Volunteer Movement, but the problem of the British Army was to remain for several years more. Indeed it required another war, in which we were not actively engaged but vitally interested, to begin the march towards change.

The humiliation of France, the entry of the Germans into Paris in 1871, and the harsh peace terms they dictated, indicated that the balance of power in Europe had been thrust violently eastwards, and that henceforth Prussia, and not France, must be No. 1 preoccupation for British politicians and militarists. Three years earlier Gladstone had become Prime Minister for the first time. As Chancellor of the Exechequer for many years he had always been extremely critical of military expenditure; as a Liberal he opposed the tendency towards increasing armaments; and as a moral politician was determined to do all he could to wipe out corruption. For these and other reasons he included in his first Cabinet as Secretary for War a young, enterprising and progressive politician, with the main tasks of reorganising the War Office and the Army. Edward Cardwell had entered the House of Commons in his twenties, and was now a fine, vigorous reformer, who wasted no time in tackling the problems. How big these problems were may be gauged from the fact that one of his reforms was the abolition, at a cost of £7,000,000 of commissions by purchase, which had persisted for many years despite constant criticism. The practice had resulted in the existence in the Army of minors, ne'er-do-wells and others totally unfitted and in many cases unable to train soldiers and lead them into battle.

The Crimean War was exceptional in that it was the biggest commitment our land and sea forces had had since Waterloo or were to have until the South African War. It was also one of the outstanding instances, even in British history, of bungling leadership in the field and criminal negligence behind the lines. The only good result of the Crimean adventure was that it opened the public's eyes to the corrupt state of the Army and its ancillary services, and created an insistent demand for reform. For many years, for a long time before the Napoleonic Wars, the Army had contained at one end of the scale officers who held rank not because of their ability but because they had bought commissions or had powerful patrons: and at the other end privates recruited from the lowest classes, often incapable of being properly trained, and in whom discipline could be instilled only by bullying and flogging. For these reasons and others the Regular Army had never been popular, even in war, and in the long years of peace its credit with the public sank lower and lower. High living and laxity in the officers' mess, fraud and corruption in the commissariat, ordnance and supply departments, and the harsh discipline of the barrack square, combined to produce an Army which cost far more than it was worth and lacked the leadership and spirit for great achievements. In those degenerate days there were many reasons for joining the Army, mostly far removed from a burning desire to serve one's country. A man who disliked regular work, dodged his responsibilities as a citizen or as a family man, was disappointed in love or had fallen foul of the law, could take the Queen's shilling and get away from it all. There was also the category of the foolish yokels who, befuddled by beer bought by the recruiting sergeant, or charmed by the rosy pictures painted of the joys of soldiering, had signed away their freedom and realised too late the real misery and degradation of being a soldier. It was in the shadow of this dark reputation that Cardwell prepared his plan of reform.

One of his major problems was how to co-ordinate the various activities of the Service and bring them under the control of the War Office, thus making himself not only completely in charge of Army affairs but also alone responsible for the machine and answerable in Parliament for any shortcomings. Great efficiency and lower costs were the twin targets, at first sight incompatible but really interdependent. It had been self-evident, during the Crimean War that the machine as it stood was broken down and badly in need of repair and reconstruction.

At that time (of the Crimean War) the whole organisation of the military forces of Britain, in the field and at the desk, was so decentralised as to be ridiculously unco-ordinated. The Commander-in-Chief was technically at the head of the armed forces and directly responsible to the King so far as the activities of the army were concerned. He also advised the King regarding commissions. But he had to defer to the Secretary for War and the Colonies in matters of finance, although such finance applied only to the pay of his forces. There were independent departments covering ordnance and engineering, and the commissariat department was under the wing and subject to the control of the

Treasury. For full measure the Home Secretary's department was responsible for the Militia. The Secretary at War came into action only in the event of war—a curious state of affairs which it took a war to alter. In 1854 the Colonial Office and the War Office were separated, and in the following year the Secretary of State for War and the Secretary at War became one and the same person. After that it was a mere matter of time before other bits of streamlining were effected. The commissariat, engineering and ordnance sections were included, as they always should have been, in the orbit of the War Office.

There was still one point which needed reform. The Commander-in-Chief, in his office at the Horse Guards, was responsible for all the daily activities of the military machine. The Secretary for War, whose office was immediately opposite on the other side of Whitehall, was responsible for the political use of that machine and for keeping it in running order. In 1870 even this demarcation line was abolished. The two administrations were merged under the control of the Secretary for War, and this system remained constant until 1965 when the Ministry of Defence was given overall control of and responsibility for the three fighting services.

One of the suggested remedies for the parlous state of our defences was the introduction of conscription. The success of the Prussian arms was regarded by some Government advisers as due to the efficient use of men called to the Colours by age groups, thoroughly trained as soldiers and then placed in reserve, ready for action if required. It might have been argued on the other side that the French had had conscription since the days of Napoleon, and the system had not helped them a great deal in 1870–71. The Prussians were top dogs in Europe not because they had conscription, but because they had developed the science of war to a greater extent than their rivals, and were imbued with a much greater passion for victory and conquest. They were in the ascendant; the French nation, militarily speaking, was in a state of decadence; and the result was Sedan and all that followed. There were several reasons, apart from the opposition of Gladstone and his chief ministers, for the unpopularity of the conscription idea. One was the traditional belief that the Royal Navy was the bulwark of defence, and that no enemy could set foot on British soil without first defeating the Navy—an unthinkable occurrence. Another factor was the age-old British antipathy to large standing armies, an antipathy which dated from Stuart and Cromellian times. A third and very potent reason was that any kind of compulsory service by age groups would entail a great rise in expenditure on the armed forces, and more economy, not more spending, was the need. Any comparison with the Continental nations was refuted by the anti-conscriptionists as not valid, since Britain had no long land frontiers to fortify and patrol, and therefore was free from the danger of a sudden inroad by a neighbouring nation.

Compulsion being ruled out, the alternatives to be considered were a revival of the Militia on the old lines, the development of the highly successful volunteer movement, or a combination of both. Cardwell realised that the existence of a really strong Volunteer Force integrated with the Regular Army and following, so far as possible, Regular Army training, would be a valuable addition to our forces in time of war, and not bear too heavily on the Exchequer in time of peace. So he decided on the third alternative and based his estimates for the Budget of 1871 on a military organisation with five distinct branches—Regular Army, an Army Reserve, the Militia, the Yeomanry and the Volunteers. At an estimated expenditure of £15,851,700 for the year he visualised an army of nearly half a million men, made up as follows:

Regular Army:	135,000 (at home and abroad)
First Army Reserves:	9,000
Second Army Reserves:	30,000 (mainly pensioners)
Militia:	139,000
Yeomanry:	14,000
Volunteers:	170,000
	497,000

It will be noticed that the Volunteers and Yeomanry together outnumbered the Regular Army and Reserves, and that each group was larger than the Militia. The most important reform was that the whole force was to come under the direct control of the War Office. For this reason the Lords-Lieutenant lost their autonomous rights to organise and raise volunteer corps in their respective counties; and the Queen's Commission, whether for the Regular Army, the Militia or the voluntary forces, could no longer be the subject of sale, barter, or the whims and fancies of local favouritisms and prejudices. In co-ordinating the entire forces of the Crown on a national basis Cardwell was foreshadowing the larger reforms that took place a generation later and resulted in the formation of the Territorial Force. Cardwell had two objects—the encouragement of local enthusiasm and the construction of a network of military establishments covering the whole country but controlled from Whitehall. At the same time his reforms led to great improvements in the conditions of service with the Regulars, so that the standard of the recruit grew higher and the efficiency of the line regiments improved.

While the idea of the county regiment was not abandoned, the Cardwell plan provided for greater cohesion. The country was divided into districts, each having a line regiment of two battalions, one serving at home and the other abroad; and Militia and Volunteers battalions linked with the Regulars. This plan, it will be seen, formed the basis for the foundation of the Territorial Force in 1907, when each infantry regiment consisted not only of the two regular battalions but also a third battalion of Special Reservists, and two more battalions, the fourth and fifth, composed entirely of Volunteers.

It was perhaps typical of the British way of doing things that these and many other reforms, dictated to a great extent by public disquiet under the threat of war, should be achieved as the country became once more comparatively free from danger from abroad. Our troops still garrisoned many places overseas, and "local incidents" were of frequent occurrence, but the real effect of the Cardwell reforms was the achievement of an efficient army system at the lowest possible cost, and a co-ordination of all the armed land forces of the Crown, including volunteers. When the new machine was in full working order its separate yet interdependent functions were clear—the Regulars to serve at home and abroad, the Militia to make good wastages in the Regular ranks, and the Volunteers and Yeomanry to help in maintaining public order and repelling invading forces. Inevitably in the absence of an invading army, which had not been in the realm of possibility since Napoleon's day, the "active service" of the Volunteers was limited to domestic affairs, and it has already been shown that the authorities were never reluctant to employ the part-time soldier in this way.

In 1873 the Mobilisation Committee recommended that the Volunteer Force should be amalgamated with the Regular Army, and to consider this and other matters the Secretary for War appointed in 1878 a Committee, under the chairmanship of Lord Bury, M.P., to go into the whole question of reviving the Volunteer Force. This Committee made many wise recommendations and signed off with these words:

"It (the Volunteer Force) has increased from year to year in numbers, and has cheerfully answered every call made on it for increased efficiency. Regard being had to its number and condition, it is probably as inexpensive a force for the protection of the State as any that could be devised; and it contains within itself the means of indefinite expansion."

14

IT is time to consider the part played by sailors in the volunteer movement, and to observe that, while some form of voluntary recruiting for H.M. ships had always existed, it was not until the middle of the 19th century that any organised system existed.

The first naval equivalent of the volunteer infantry were the Coastal Fencibles, founded during the Napoleonic Wars for the defence of coast, ports and the Martello towers erected on the east and southern shores of Britain. But although recruited mainly from fishermen, retired seamen and other nautical types they were land-based and neither expected nor were required to go afloat in war vessels. They were also exempt from the claims of the press-gangs, and so were able to go about their ordinary callings, whether in fishing boats or in shore employments, while training for their defensive duties. It seems strange that men who were well qualified to sail ships and, in many cases, to fight ships' guns, should be exempt from that kind of activity, while in the seaports and the inland towns and villages men of little or no fighting experience should be forcibly enrolled in the Navy.

In 1852, after the Duke of Wellington had sounded the alarm regarding the national defences (see Chapter XI), the first real attempt to form an official body of naval volunteers was made. This force, the Royal Naval Coast Volunteers, was formed from seafaring men who, unlike the Coastal Fencibles of fifty years before, contracted to serve afloat if required, but not more than 150 miles from British shores. In various administrative respects the new body was akin to the land militia, with a service period of five years, pay on military scales, and exemption from compulsory service with the Navy. And since most of the 10,000 recruits were fishermen, their training was arranged so as to leave them free for following their employment in the fishing season.

At first the R.N.C.V. was under the control of the Coastguard Service, members of which gave instruction in the use of rifles and naval artillery. In 1856 the Admiralty assumed control but three years later, in response to a demand of senior naval officers for a force of experienced retired naval men, the Royal Naval Reserve was formed. The rapid development of the R.N.R. led to the practical extinction of the R.N.C.V. and in 1872, numbering less than 1,000 men, the Corps changed its title and became the Royal Navy Artillery Volunteers. It existed, cinderella-like, for another nineteen years, when it was disbanded at the insistence of Admiralty critics who did not hide their dislike of what they regarded as a collection of unseamanlike volunteers.

Those criticisms had long since been forgotten when another generation of tradesmen and professional men did their bit in the 1914-18 war and earned battle honours at Antwerp, Zeebrugge and elsewhere. But we must now consider the onset of an earlier war, how it resulted in volunteer soldiers fighting overseas, caused the flame of enthusiasm to burn at its brightest, and paved the way to the fullest possible recognition of volunteers as an integral part of the military system of the country.

The debate on Naval volunteers in 1891 was one of the few occasions, since the completion of Cardwell's army reforms in 1871, that the volunteer movement had come under public notice. The intervening twenty years had been a period of peace, at least for the great majority of the inhabitants of the British Isles. Few were touched by the effects of war and conflict. British soldiers lost their lives fighting in foreign parts, in the Ashanti incident of 1873 and the Afghanistan war of 1878, but the loss of 700 lives in the *Princess Alice* steamer disaster of 1878 was of much greater concern to the British public. The Zulu war of 1879 was as nothing compared with the Tay Bridge disaster. And the Sudan war was soon forgotten in the celebrations in 1887 for Queen Victoria's Golden Jubilee. There seemed to be no cloud on the horizon.

The British Empire was expanding as one annexation after another was made by British diplomacy or British arms, and prosperity as well as peace ruled at home. Yet the following year, 1888, marked the beginning of a change, although apart from public mourning for the Emperor William I of Prussia and the Emperor Frederick of Austria, who had died within a few months of each other, these events had no significance for the man in the street. Two years later the opening of the Forth Bridge took precedence in the public mind over the dismissal of Bismarck, the Iron Chancellor, by a Kaiser who was already dreaming of world conquest. And what concern was it to the ordinary British man or woman that Heligoland, an insignificant lump of rock in the North Sea, had been ceded to Germany?

So Britain went into the naughty nineties, while abroad the German war plans went ahead and in other lands democratic influences were at work. Even while gay crowds celebrated in 1897 Her Majesty's Diamond Jubilee, the complacent Victorian world had begun, the slow descent from the peak.

For many years the political situation in South Africa had caused friction between the Afrikaaners and the British. Successive colonisation moves led to the complete encirclement of the Transvaal by Portuguese and British possessions and protectorates; and various trials of strength between President Kruger on the one hand and Cecil Rhodes and the British Government on the other merely served to render a dangerous situation critical. The abortive Jameson Raid in 1895 was followed by political moves, including a military union between the Transvaal and the Orange Free State, and events gradually escalated until Kruger's ultimatum and the start of the South African War on October 12th, 1899. There had been much popular support in Britain for "teaching those Boers a lesson". The word "jingoism" was added to the language by the defiant and confident lines:

> "We don't want to fight, but, by jingo! if we do
> We've got the ships, we've got the men, we've got
> the money, too."

These were words well suited to the popular attitude, but they were very far from reflecting the actual situation. Britain, as

as it transpired, did not have "the men", not at least in sufficient
numbers for the job. Possession of ships and money did not in
itself guarantee success, and it was soon to be proved that staff
work and forward thinking were inadequate. Public enthusiasm,
indeed, was far from being matched by official zeal in planning
for and prosecuting the war; and in retrospect we can see that
Britain has scarcely ever entered a major conflict so ill-prepared
as she was in October 1899.

When hostilities started, British forces in South Africa numbered just over 20,000, half of these having been fetched from
India when it was seen that war with Kruger's Transvaal was
practically inevitable. On the outbreak of war the British Government ordered the formation of an Army Corps to be sent out
under Sir Redvers Buller, then C. in C. Aldershot, but the stark
fact was that the parlous state of our military forces after years
without a major conflict made it extremely difficult to provide the
50,000 men required, fully trained and equipped. There was little
or no hope of withdrawing regular forces from abroad—even the
10,000 Sir George White had taken to Natal had seriously weak-
ened our garrisons in India; and racial problems made unthinkable
any idea of using native troops from the Empire against the Boers.
There were offers from the Colonies of white volunteers, but
while some of these were accepted the military men at home still
believed that the affair could be handled exclusively by Regulars.
In view of the fact that the Regular Reserves had to be called on
before Buller's Army Corps could be completed, this belief
seemed to be just another instance of the official capacity for leaving things to chance. So the Regulars who had been trained on the
barrack square in the methods and traditions of Inkerman and
Sebastopol were joined by reservists short of training, and
together they set off in the wake of their commander for a war
that was to be far removed from their conception of war. Composed nine-tenths of infantry trained to use rifles from deployed
positions, to stand firm against charges, and to obey *en masse* the
tactical commands of their leaders, they were about to have a
painful initiation into a mounted war of movement against a
will-o'-the-wisp enemy who would not stand and fight it out but

would prefer to sting at long range by stealth and subterfuge. There was nothing unfair about the Boer tactics—conceding the supposition that all is fair in war. They adopted methods and strategems suited to their way of life and the terrain over which they fought. The British errors were to assume, against all available evidence, that the campaign would be fought under Wellingtonian rules; neglecting to obtain or act on the advice of white South Africans who knew the country and the Boers; and failing to profit by the lessons learned in the early part of the campaign. Perfecting the art of the new warfare was a long and tragic process, and many braves lives were lost and more than one reputation sullied before the situation was brought under control. In the meantime the last three months of 1899 had produced reverse after reverse, with British forces fighting to rule proving quite unable to contain the widely-scattered and free-roving Boers, falling into trap after trap, and suffering sometimes ten times more casualties than their elusive foes.

For these reasons British fortunes, both militarily and politically, had never been lower than they were in the last week of 1899 and the first few of 1900. The battle of Colenso on December 15th had cost Buller ten guns and 1,100 casualties; his Boer attackers had scarcely been touched, and he himself was dispirited by the disastrous culmination of this "Black Week" of reverses. It was a week that left Britain stunned and her enemies scornful. The complacent Victorian myth had been exploded. The rulers of an Empire on which the sun never set had reached the nadir of humiliation. And over the European horizon hung a huge question mark. If a party of Boer farmers, fighting more or less as individuals and not embarrassed by the absence of Army discipline, beat the best troops Britain put in the field, how could the Home Country hope to foil the ambitions of Germany, Russia, or France?

Not surprisingly the final defeat of Buller at Colenso brought to a head the British public's dissatisfaction with the conduct of the war. The Government under Lord Salisbury appointed Field-Marshal Lord Roberts of Kandahar, whose only son had been killed at Colenso, to be Commander-in-Chief in South Africa, and gave him as chief of staff Lord Kitchener of Khartoum. These appointments met with general approval. They seemed to exemplify the spirit of defiance in the face of adversity which, in the long British history, has often followed early reverses for our arms. But although "Bobs" and "K. of K." carried the confidence of a populace far too easily swayed by the treacly sentimentality of those late Victorian times, anyone intimately acquainted with the manpower situation was far from happy.

The forces available to Buller when he began operations early in November 1899 could not have numbered more than 50,000 men, a total which grew in the next few weeks to about 80,000, but by the end of the Colenso battle this number had been seriously depleted by losses in killed and wounded and the many prisoners in the hands of the Boers. There was, too, a heavy incidence of disease. The War Office was therefore faced with the task of not only repairing the wastage, but also expanding the forces hitherto considered sufficient for the job. All available reserves were called up and hurried arrangements made to repair glaring deficiencies in training, equipment and armaments. The Militia was combed for men able and willing to serve in battle. There was an appeal for recruits for the Regular Army which was answered with a fair degree of enthusiasm. But the unpleasant fact remained that with all these efforts there was still a grave shortage of manpower, in view of the delicate situation at the front and the possibility that the conflict might drag on for a long time. So far Whitehall had not looked beyond the Regular Army and its reserves, reinforced by what could be obtained from the Militia. Another division was raised for service in South Africa but Britain was now virtually starved of trained men, and the authorities, rather reluctantly, agreed to formulate a plan for recruiting volunteers and yeomanry for war service. In this way, under the impact of the December reverses and the threat of more trouble to come, the volunteer organisations of Britain began to play their historic part.

Even in this extremity the Government's habit of caution and parsimony could not be thrown aside. There was a call for young men who could ride horses. They were formed into the Imperial

Yeomanry—a move which was regarded as essential, since even the most hidebound adherents of warfare of the Crimean variety had now to admit that Buller's reverses had been due partly to his lack of mobility and forced reliance on infantry. Horses were going to count a great deal in future operations, but the Government were not disposed to supply mounts for the young men who came forward in their thousands to join the Imperial Yeomanry. All of them had to supply their own horses and equipment, or be mounted and equipped by patriotic and wealthy sponsors. This led to the formation of many troops of Yeomanry who bore the names of their sponsors into battle.

The early reverses of our arms in South Africa were due not least to the complete failure of politicians and generals to realise that the war would not be a conflict between conventional forces drawn up in battle array, but a campaign of hide-and-seek. The British Army in India, the Sudan and other parts had had plenty of experience in dealing with natives of various races, and had found that superior fire power and more intelligent organisation brought success. But the opposing forces in the South African war were not untaught, untrained natives armed with spears. They were white men who had learned many lessons the hard way in dealing with the Kaffirs, and had the intelligence and the power to put those lessons to good account in defying the Queen's armies.

The way of life of the Boers, living on scattered farms and forced to be constantly on guard against marauding natives and savage beasts, had made them accustomed to the strategy of the veldt—the sudden raid, the hurried defence, the stealthy sortie and the quick retreat. Their weapon was the rifle and their transport the horse, their commissariat the saddle bag, their bivouac the open veldt, their tactics to hit and run so that they might fight another day. To all these self-reliant factors was added a will to co-operate—the ability to combine when the magnitude of the danger demanded united action. The individual Boer farmer barricaded his house and armed his family against hostile Kaffirs. And if the attack exceeded the proportions of a local raid on his cattle the farmers of a whole district would assemble as a commando to defend the territory and their united families.

Tactics which had proved successful against the natives were employed with surprising success against the British troops, particularly in the principal battles of Buller's campaign. During the succeeding campaign of Roberts better staff work, a keener appreciation of Boer tactics, and superiority in manpower and fire-power, almost ended the war within eight months; but De Wet and others who succeeded Kruger used commando tactics with such skill and desperation that fighting dragged on for nearly two more years. Eventually we found the answer to the problem, but many weary months of fighting, and thousands of casualties through wounds and disease, would have been saved if there had been intelligent staff work and far-seeing generalship from the start.

Simultaneously with the appointment of Lord Roberts and Lord Kitchener the Government adopted measures to remedy the critical manpower situation. The remainder of the 1st Army Reserve so far uncommitted was mobilized, the production and transport of arms and artillery speeded up. In addition nine militia battalions were mobilized for service overseas, and steps taken to organize volunteers in Britain and from the Colonies. By this time it was clear that horsemen were going to be at least as important as infantry in this unusual type of warfare—hence the call for yeomanry volunteers for active service and the invitation to the Colonies. If the War Office had been able to foresee in October the situation as it existed three months later more official heed might have been taken of the many offers of volunteer services made at the start of the war. But under-estimation of the opposition and complacent satisfaction with an entirely unsatisfactory manpower position had so warped official judgment that none of these suggestions was even considered until the full impact of "Black Week" spurred Whitehall to action.

There had been dozens of offers from men of substance and station who would have raised many contingents at no public expense if the Government had given the word; and many hundreds of individuals were ready and willing to serve in South Africa. Sir Horace Vincent of the Queen's Westminsters and Colonel Balfour of the London Scottish were among the commanders of volunteer infantry regiments who offered to raise special battalions. Lord Lonsdale was prepared not only to raise and equip 1,000 volunteer Yeomanry at his own expense, but also to pay the cost of transporting them to the front. There was also a suggestion that a number of Yeomanry units should combine to raise a representative force. Another proposal, which was pressed in many influential quarters without success, was that the Government should implement a clause in an Act of 1895 which allowed Volunteers to come forward for active service whenever the Militia was embodied. The general official attitude was that the situation did not justify taking any step save those within the compass of the Regular Army and the Militia. And even when Government sanction was given to the recruitment of Volunteers and Yeomanry for service overseas it was seen by many officials as less a contribution to the military strength of Lord Roberts's forces than a safety valve for the upsurge of enthusiasm among the citizens of the Empire.

This cynical, blasé attitude led the Government to deal with the matter in so lukewarm and parsimonious a manner that a tremendous amount of keenness was dissipated for want of funds and official encouragement. Lack of money, a dearth of training facilities, a shortage of instructors and up-to-date equipment, and much wasteful competition between Government and private sponsors for the acquisition of horses, kept down the number of volunteers to perhaps less than quarter of what would have been possible if the matter had been properly handled. Soon after Colenso the War Office grudgingly decided to recruit 3,000 volunteer Yeomanry for South Africa to be paid as cavalry and equipped and mounted by the Government. By the end of January 1,500 of these were on their way to South Africa. Twice that number sailed in February, a further 3,500 in March, and by the end of April 10,500 British Imperial Yeomanry were fighting alongside Regular troops. A strong committee under Colonel Lucas had been formed to co-ordinate the Yeomanry effort and the Committee's offices in London were kept busy dealing with applications from citizens of every class and occupation. Clerks and farmers jostled with businessmen and lawyers. Members of both Houses of Parliament vied with hawkers and cab-drivers for the privilege of riding to war for the sake of King and Country. The majority of applicants had experience of horses, but many applied in the hope that they would receive instruction and so be able to serve. But it was impossible to take non-riders. Even if there had been instructors to spare no time was available.

In addition to the Imperial Yeomanry detachments, which were attached to different regiments as mounted riflemen as and when they arrived in South Africa, a number of independent units of Yeomanry were formed by individuals. Lord Donoughmore raised the Duke of Cambridge's Own, and Lord Loch a battalion of men with experience of South Africa. The 18th Battalion (Sharpshooters), 19th Battalion (Paget's Horse) and the 20th Battalion (Roughriders) were raised respectively by the Earl of Dunraven, Mr. George Paget and Lord Lathom. There was a company from Manchester and six from Ireland. One of the most interesting of these privately-sponsored units was Lovat's Scouts, consisting mainly of tenants and workers from the Scottish estates of Lord Lovat, and therefore men accustomed to the skills and the difficulties of deer stalking and hard riding, and also inured to bad weather. They were in their element in South Africa, where the veldt and kopjes were not unlike the moors and hills of their native land; and the Boers learned to respect foes who understood their tactics.

There were limits to the number of men who could be taken into the Yeomanry—limits imposed by considerations already mentioned. But another outlet for patriotic enthusiasm was provided. The War Office decided to apply the Imperial Yeomanry principle to the Volunteers, i.e., the raising of composite units by taking volunteers from existing units. The biggest of these, and one which for other reasons gained tremendous prestige, was the City Imperial Volunteers. Lord Lansdowne, Secretary for War, was approached by the Lord Mayor of London, Sir Arthur Newton, and others with an offer by the City to raise, equip and convey to South Africa, at no expense to the Government, a corps of 1,000 men from the London Volunteer

Companies. The offer was of course accepted gladly, and in a short time everything was being done at great speed and with tremendous enthusiasm. The £100,000 required for the venture was subscribed in a matter of days, the City Corporation putting down £15,000 and business houses and individuals contributing the rest. In addition two shipping companies (Union Castle and Wilson's of Hull) offered to transport between them the 1,000 men free of charge. The only mistake the sponsors made in these preliminaries was to set their target too low. The keenness to join excelled all expectations. No fewer than forty-seven Volunteer companies answered the call, and it was soon apparent that the arbitrary quota of twenty from each company was far below the number who pressed for inclusion. In some cases double that number came forward, and the planned 1,000 men became 1,740, all of whom embarked at Southampton in five vessels during the third week of January 1900. Only a month had passed since the idea was born.

Four hundred of the men went as mounted infantry, and there was also a battery of 12½-pounder Vickers-Maxim quick-firing guns, donated by the manufacturers and manned almost entirely by H.A.C. personnel. The commanding officer of the C.I.V. was Colonel W. H. Mackinnon and under him Major the Earl of Albemarle commanded the infantry, Major H. C. Cholmondeley the mounted infantry, and Major G. McMicking the Battery. It was obvious from the response that if the authorities had been more helpful with advice, facilities and money, the C.I.V. would have doubled or trebled its numbers. But the City of London had done its bit.

In the country at large similar preparations were made, exemplifying the keenness of the volunteers and also the unyielding attachment of authority to rules and regulations. It was decided that service companies of Volunteers should be formed and attached to regular regiments on arrival in South Africa, as had been done with the Yeomanry. But many men were lost to the scheme because the plan was inelastic. Some companies could have given twice their quota and more—there were even instances of companies volunteering en bloc—but this could not be allowed.

So the total strength of the service companies which went to South Africa during Lord Roberts's campaign was under 10,000. There were some additions later, and during the whole war 26,000, including the C.I.V. and the Imperial Yeomanry, were involved.

The number of volunteers in South Africa was considerably augmented by irregular corps raised on the spot from among British citizens living there, and also Colonials and even foreign sympathisers, including a group of Texan cowboys who brought their own horses. The British regulars called these local units "scallywags", and perhaps in the use of that term there was something of the good-natured contempt with which a Royal Navy man regards a "tramp". But whatever contempt there might have been soon changed into affection, for the scallywags played their parts and fought as well as units of regular lineage. One Colonial unit that was composed of nearly 600 roughriders from the far west of Canada, raised, equipped and sent to South Africa entirely at his own expense by Lord Strathcona, Canadian High Commissioner and Governor of the Hudson's Bay Company.

One of the most successful of the units raised in South Africa itself was a mounted corps composed of members of the Caledonian Society of Johannesburg. In no time at all four squadrons were in action and their commander, the Marquis of Tullibardine, decided to call for more volunteers from Scots at home and in the Colonies. The response was so great that 400 men went from Scotland and 250 from Australia alone among the overseas detachments. This corps subsequently became the Scottish Horse and as such was incorporated into the Territorial Force, with headquarters at Aberdeen. A corps of mounted rifles was also recruited from Johannesburg residents. The first irregular unit to be actively engaged was the Imperial Light Horse, formed at Natal. The latest was probably the South African Light Horse, which was really a collection of units on the Imperial Yeomanry lines, and did great service and suffered heavy losses at Colenso. There were also Brabant's Horse, formed by Colonel E. Brabant from Eastern Province farmers; Colonel Bayly's Horse, Colonel Nezbitt's Horse and Mr. Orpen's Horse. All these, and other irregular forces, were eventually formed into a Colonial Division, and Colonel Brabant, promoted Major-General, was given the command.

We must now return to the C.I.V., who, with Government-issued rifles and ammunition but everything else supplied from the Lord Mayor's fund, arrived in South Africa after scarcely any time in which to settle down as a cohesive unit. There was a heterogeneous collection of uniforms—grey, green, black, red, blue—but in one factor at least they were united—the will to work hard and fight hard. By the middle of February they were ready to leave Cape Town and proceed towards the front, behind which they had six weeks' hard training. From then on it was the real thing and their first big test under their commander, Colonel Mackinnon, was in the battle of Doornkop, part of the British offensive against Pretoria, where they operated in the 21st Brigade under General Bruce Hamilton. General H. Smith-Dorrien in his despatch on this battle, had this to say about the part played by the C.I.V.:

"The features of the day were the attacks of the Gordon High-landers and the C.I.V. That of the C.I.V. convinced me that this corps . . . is as skilled as the most skilful of our regulars at skirmishing. The men were handled with the most consummate skill by Colonel Mackinnon, Col. Lord Albemarle, and their other officers, and it was entirely due to this skill and the quickness and dash of their movements, and taking advantage of every fold in the ground, that, in spite of a terrific fire from several direc-tions, they drove the enemy from several positions with com-paratively small loss."

Months afterwards, when the now seasoned C.I.V. was re-viewed by Lord Roberts (Oct. 2nd, 1900) the men heard the great soldier full of praise for their performances. "The admirable work performed by the C.I.V., the volunteers now attached to regular battalions, and the Imperial Yeomanry, have, I rejoice to say, proved that I was right, and that England, relying as she does on the patriotic volunteer system for their defence, is resting on no broken reed."

Hard on the heels of the C.I.V. infantry their artillery arrived in South Africa towards the end of February 1900. The guns were manned mostly by members of the Honourable Artillery Company, drawn by London omnibus horses, and did excellent work throughout the campaign.

The time-honoured conception of a cavalry man with lance and sabre went with the wind of change which came with the South African war. Some forty regiments of volunteer cavalry contributed to the Imperial Yeomanry, and no doubt some individuals were disappointed that, by Government order, they were to be armed with rifles and bayonets instead of swords and carbines, and were to become mounted riflemen. This was a necessity in view of the conditions of war in South Africa, but it complicated the preparation of these volunteer horsemen for the front. They had to add to the skills already learned; and foot drill, firing practice and bayonet exercise had to be assimilated, to say nothing of camp drills and the care and accommodation of horses on active service.

There were some events, nevertheless, which did not find a place in the new training manual for mounted infantry, which had just been issued but which the Yeomanry volunteers had had no time to study. There was, for example, the case of the mules from the Argentine. Always during the campaign the cry was for horses. And in such circumstances a lot of the horseflesh sent to South Africa by dealers and others intent on profiting by the business was not fit for the job. In such a critical movement as Roberts's advance across the Modder River towards Johannesburg the Imperial Yeomanry were anxiously awaiting horses which had been promised for the job. But when the beasts arrived they proved to be Argentine mules. They had spent some three weeks on the boat and then some days on the train covering the 600 miles from Cape Town. It was anybody's guess whether they had been broken in before despatch. What was certain was that the voyage and the train journey had removed what little discipline might have been implanted in them in their native land. And these unruly creatures were handed over to the Yeomanry, who were supposed to saddle them, bestride them and use them in an important tactical movement in support of the infantry.

The result was chaos. There was an hour or two of wild excitement of a rodeo-like description, and the infantry got under way leaving the veldt littered with saddlery and dotted with frantic would-be riders trying to round up rebellious won't-be-ridden mules. This, as related to me by Colonel R. T. Lang of the South African War Veterans' Association, might be regarded as an amusing sidelight on that war; but at the time it must have been seen as just another example of lack of staff work.

In spite of these and other mishaps, which they accepted with a philosophy which would have done credit to any old sweat, the Volunteers and the Yeomanry gave grand service to the Commander-in-Chief during six months of hard fighting which, so everyone thought, had seen the end of any serious Boer resistance. And one of the last acts of Lord Roberts before he asked to be recalled to Britain was to send home these part-time soldiers who had served him so well.

Erskine Childers, who left his job as Clerk to the House of Commons to volunteer for South Africa, gave an interesting personal account of his adventures as a driver with the H.A.C. Battery in the C.I.V., when he wrote *In the Ranks of the C.I.V.* The H.A.C., it is clear, had no need to use mules from the Argentine or from any other doubtful source, because they took 114 horses out with them, lost only four on the voyage and handed over ninety-four to the remount department before leaving South Africa. The H.A.C. Battery was in General H. A. Paget's Division and their C.O. had this to say to Major McMicking and his men when the Battery left for Cape Town on the way home:

"Lord Roberts has decided to send you home and I have come to say goodbye and to express my regret at having to part with you. In its many engagements the C.I.V. has always done its work well. Owing to the excellent practice made by your guns you have the satisfaction of knowing that you have been the cause of great savings of lives in the Infantry and at times the Cavalry." After dealing in detail with several actions in which the smart and skilful work of the C.I.V. guns had helped towards success, General Paget concluded: "I am sorry to lose you. There is more hard work to be done; and you cannot realise what it is to me to lose a body of men whom I knew I could always rely upon. You are returning home to receive a hearty welcome which you undoubtedly deserve."

Before leaving Pretoria the C.I.V. Infantry, the Imperial Yeomanry Mounted Infantry and the volunteer Batteries were reviewed by Lord Roberts, who was accompanied by all his staff. In his speech of farewell Bobs said he hoped they would carry home to the heart of the country a high opinion of the regular British soldier alongside whom they had fought.

On November 27th, almost eight months since they had sailed on the great adventure, the C.I.V. had a tremendous welcome from the citizens of London. But this was merely the culmination of a welcoming wave which had started rolling at Southampton, where vast crowds swarmed to the quayside to watch the men embark. And all along the line the wayside stations were filled with people waving flags and cheering as the train bore the volunteers to London, to another crazy welcome at Paddington, to a march through crowded streets and to a service of thanksgiving at St. Paul's Cathedral.

Lord Roberts's remark about the regular British soldier was not lost upon these returning heroes. Childers recalled that even at this moment of triumph and gratitude "we had a thought in the background of a dusty khaki figure still plodding the distant veldt —our friend and our comrade, Atkins, who had done more and bloodier work than we, and who is not at the end of it yet." Prophetic words, indeed. Much more than another year was to pass before the British Tommy's work was finished in South Africa.

As an experiment the C.I.V. was a great success, and the Imperial Yeomanry also proved to be a tremendously valuable force, particularly in a war fought so largely on horseback. But most of the volunteers who rallied to the call in that winter of 1899–1900 were attached to regular regiments from their districts, and this integration of volunteers with regulars was bound to be to the advantage of both. The system, indeed, foreshadowed the Haldane plan for the reconstruction of our military forces, each regiment consisting of Regulars, Militia and Volunteers in their separate battalions, but sharing the same command, the same spirit and the same kind of training.

Some of the official apathy regarding the volunteers was due perhaps to the public attitude towards "men playing at soldiers" which had persisted all through the years of peace. Lord French, who as Major-General John French commanded the cavalry in South Africa, wrote many years afterwards that the Volunteers and Yeomanry rebutted by their fighting spirit, their courage, their ability and their soldierly bearing the ill-conceived criticisms which they had endured before the war. Later Lord French was to wax even more eulogistically about the performances of the Territorials who helped to prevent the overrunning of Northern France by the Kaiser's armies at the start of World War I.

The fact was that the Volunteers and Yeomanry had "played soldiers" for generations before they faced the real thing in South Africa. They had been called out occasionally to put down civil strife and assist the authorities in keeping the peace at home. They had taken part in reviews and manœuvres alongside Regular Army units. They had worked hard to perfect themselves in the art of war and the use of weapons. But not until the Volunteers and the Imperial Yeomanry faced the Boers in South Africa had men outside the Regular Army and the Militia passed through the test of battle. That they came through many of these tests to the satisfaction of everyone, including the highest Army leaders, was the dusty answer of the volunteers to the scorn and ridicule to which they had been subjected in peacetime.

There was no doubt about the almost hysterical praise which was lavished on the homecoming volunteers by the public, and the generals were sincere in their approbation. There were medals, too, to commemorate this first major adventure overseas by British volunteers. But these and other tokens of admiration and gratitude were not accompanied by practical official help for the heroes and their dependents. Thousands of young men, many of them leaving behind wives, children, or aged parents, went off to South Africa with no guarantee of any recompense for good service, compensation for incapacitation, or security for dependents if they failed to return. They went mostly with no other thoughts than those connected with a sense of adventure and an urge to fight for their country. If any did wonder what might happen to themselves and dependents if they were killed or incapacitated by wounds they may have assumed that a grateful Goverment would take care of such eventualities. Such assumptions, if they existed at all, would have been proved far too optimistic. The Government in fact did next to nothing. The Welfare State had not yet arrived. There was no Ministry of Pensions, no scheme of National Insurance. This was the Victorian era, in which poverty meant starvation and to be destitute was a sin. The man out of work, or unable to work through injury or ill-health, had to depend for sustenance on public charity, and in the last desperate straits would exchange his miserable home for the equally miserable workhouse. For the regular soldier in those days there were married quarters, retirement pensions and compensatory pensions for wounds; but the volunteer did not qualify for any of these. There were no family allowances while these part-time soldiers were away from home, no pensions for those unable to work on their return to civilian life, and no support for the dependents of those who did not come back. It was one of several blots on our South African war record that empty phrases and useless medals were considered adequate recognition of all that volunteers in every category did and suffered in defence of the country.

The contrast between public enthusiasm and official indifference was one of the startling characteristics of this war. The enlistment of the C.I.V. and other volunteer detachments was given plenty of publicity and the newspapers were full of pictures of the men wearing their slouch hats, and of information about their preparations and movements. There was no attempt at secrecy over mobilization or the departure of troops for South Africa, and transports left Southampton in broad daylight to the waving and cheers and cries of crowds of relatives and friends left on the quayside. How different from the sealed orders, the night embarkations with doused lights, and the destroyer escorts of World War I. How different, too, was the attention paid to the soldier's welfare and the care of his dependents. In 1899–1900 there was utter neglect, so much so that the public conscience was smitten and great voluntary efforts were made to achieve what the Government would not attempt. Kipling no doubt had this situation in mind when he wrote:

"Would you kindly put a shilling in my little tambourine
For a gentleman in khaki ordered South?"

At many a concert in those days of war "The Absent-minded Beggar" was sung while little girls dressed Spanish style passed their tambourines round the audience. Collections were also made in churches for the same purpose, the offertory plates being draped in red, white and blue ribbons, because no one in those days ever missed a chance for expressing sugary sentiment.

It may be seen that the treatment of volunteers in the South African war followed a pattern we have seen repeated down the centuries. It times of emergency they were all good fellows for whom everything must be done. But as soon as the emergency was over there was indecent haste to push them into oblivion—until the next time.

15

THE South African War, beginning with many disappointments and humiliations, inspiring a revival of patriotic pride with the successful campaign of Lord Roberts, and then dragging on to a victorious but far from satisfactory conclusion, had emphasised the lack of preliminary staff work, the unjustifiable optimism of our military leaders, and the shortcomings of War Office organisation. The several reverses of Buller's campaign, the heavy casualties suffered by our regular forces which led to the call for volunteers, had been intolerable to a public accustomed to view overseas operations with detachment, imbued as everyone was with the idea that British arms were superior to those of any other country. That our professional soldiers and their generals could be outmanoeuvred, outwitted and outfought by what were little more than Boer commandos was humiliation indeed; and two long years of hard and often frustrating campaigning went on before we had thoroughly mastered the problems of this unusual conflict.

When hostilities began in October 1899 the War Office had thought it sufficient in the first place to put 20,000 men into the field pending the formation of Buller's Army Corps; and the despatch of the latter force to South Africa was generally considered to mark the end of Britain's commitments in manpower. Yet by March 1902, when peace was signed, British forces had been committed to the number of 480,000. This was easily the greatest army which had ever fought for the Home Country in any war, and the fact that it outnumbered by at least five to one the total number of Boers engaged was a measure of the difficulties the British encountered in dealing with difficult terrain, unorthodox enemy tactics and problems of communication and supply.

About one-seventh of the British forces had been recruited overseas, some 30,000 being volunteers from among British citizens in South Africa, and about the same total from Canada, Australia, New Zealand and other Colonies. As the Home Regular Forces (on paper) at the start of the War totalled 184,000 (including 78,000 in the First Reserve) it would seem that about 200,000 of those who fought under the British colours were volunteers from the Home Country. Many of these, having volunteered for the Colours, became Regulars "for the duration", but since few of them would have dreamed of joining the Army in peacetime it is right to regard them as volunteers, and so add them to the men of the Imperial Yeomanry, the City Imperial Volunteers and the special battalions attached to county regiments, most of whom were demobilised when the emergency ended and before the actual finish of the War.

Although the British losses in action were high in the first three months of the War, over the whole period they were proportionately less than those of the Boers. The total killed was 5,774 and the wounded numbered 22,829. The Boers lost 4,000 killed. But disease was the biggest killer, for no fewer than 16,000 British troops died from enteric and other maladies, attributed mainly to inefficient base organisation and inexperience of local conditions This regrettable feature of the campaign was just another result of antiquated military thinking and lack of a General Staff. Despite the Cardwell reforms initiated in the shadow of public displeasure and discontent over the revelations of inefficiency and corruption during the Crimean War, the official attitude to military procedure had not greatly changed during the last quarter of the 19th century. It is true that the Militia had been improved and the Volunteer Force placed on a firm, permanent footing; but there seemed to be no great urge to strengthen the Regular Army, in spite of worldwide evidence that our forces were becoming more and more committed to overseas service, and were likely to have graver responsibilities on the Continent. When Cardwell began his reforms the Regular Army at home numbered about 120,000. In 1899, thirty years later, the total was officially 180,000, but even this relatively small increase over so long a period did not represent the true state of affairs. The total manpower of the Line regiments on paper was 120,000, with 78,000 in the Reserves, but little more than 50 per cent. of the presumed front-line troops were ready for action, and when the South African War broke out one of the first acts of the War Office was to call up reservists to make good the deficiency. Buller's Army Corps was filled only with difficulty, and the war had been in progress eight months before the number of Regulars in South Africa reached 180,000.

This grave lack of manpower was due to many factors, including the fond illusion of many otherwise sensible men that the British Empire was supreme, that the British Navy ruled the seas and that a small standing army officered by gentlemen would always be sufficient to protect British business interests abroad and British life at home. Although we had a standing army it was an army recruited without compulsion from the State, even if there were often compelling reasons, domestic and otherwise, for men joining the Colours. The Militia Act was still in force and technically the ballot remained in existence, but only on paper, for no ballot had been operated for many years past. So in one sense anyone who wore a military uniform in Britain, whether Militiaman, Volunteer or Regular, was a volunteer. He who chose the Regular Army knew that he was pledging constant, full-time service for a number of years, to be followed by a place in the Reserves. The militia recruit knew that in an emergency he would be expected to join the Regulars "for the duration". The Volunteers and the Yeomanry were enrolled purely for home defence, mainly of a local character, and had no set terms of service.

The Regular Army had been kept at a moderate level, both in numbers and degree of training, by peacetime apathy and the tendency of successive governments to spend as little as possible on the armed forces. The emergency of 1899 showed clearly the inadequacy of our defences and the lack of a military system, and as the war dragged on it became more and more evident that the learning of the lessons was costing us dear in British lives and British prestige. In the public view, and in the opinion of forward-looking politicians and a few enlightened military leaders, our experiences in the Boer War had made imperative the need for overhauling our military structure to meet the requirements of 20th-century warfare. No one then could have had more than a premonition that the next war in which Britain was involved would be so tremendous in scale and so costly in men, money and materials as the 1914–18 conflict proved to be. But to the pressure of public opinion on general grounds in 1903 was added the realisation by deep-thinking, intelligent men that, having scrambled out of the Boer War with somewhat fly-bitten laurels, we had to prepare for a much more serious and severe test. The next time it would be not an ill-planned expedition to quell rebellious and undisciplined farmers, but involvement with one or more of the professional conscripted European armies which would demand all our energies and all the planning skill of which our leaders were capable.

For it was clear the nations of Europe were taking sides. At one time there was a distinct possibility of the balance of power in Europe being upset by a Russo-German-Franco alliance which would leave Britain almost friendless and—in the grim, vacuous aftermath of the South African War—defenceless except for her Navy. The Anglo-French treaty fortunately led to the Triple Entente and the seesaw of power politics returned to the horizontal, but Germany was now indulging to the full her ambitious aim to be the most powerful single nation in the world. The danger signals had been flying for years on the diplomatic, military and naval fronts. German politicians had made no secret of their sympathies with the Boers, had not disguised their satisfaction at British reverses and had not spared criticism of alleged ill-treatment of captured Boers and their families. The German Naval Laws of the nineties had emphasised the determination of Von Tirpitz and his Kaiser to challenge centuries-old British supremacy at sea; and the development of Germany's land forces had been the most obvious and most alarming feature of European life for the past thirty years.

In Naval matters Britain had already accepted the challenge. The first Dreadnought was on the drawing-board, and recruitment for the Navy was being speeded up, helped by the formation, in 1903, of the Royal Naval Volunteer Reserve and the Royal Marine Volunteers. No one had anything but confidence in the ability of our seamen and ships to keep ahead in the naval race. But the military problem was much more complex and for that reason progress to a satisfactory solution more difficult.

There were actually two problems—how to modernise the Regular Army and what to do with the Auxiliary forces which, by their performances in the recent war, had proved themselves indispensable. Two commissions were appointed to deal with these questions. One might have been thought enough, but whereas there was general agreement on the need for modernising the Army itself, there were many dissensions among the country's leaders, political and military, as to the composition, functions and control of the auxiliaries.

The need for a completely new approach to the organisation of our Regular forces was not in question. Our troubles in South Africa stemmed directly from the lack of a General Staff, and we went from one blunder to another, from one reverse to the next, because nothing had been planned behind the lines and no staff work done on the special problems of a South African campaign. It was easy to blame the commanders in the field and some of the blame was justified, but they were victims of lack of preparation and perception in all sectors, back to and including Whitehall. Many of our generals had apparently travelled blissfully from the Crimean War to the South African War without realising that there had been a fundamental change in the conception of war— a change that was to have far-reaching effects. The individual responsible for this change was Field Marshal Count Helmuth von Moltke, who created the modern German army and, as Chief of Staff, had been the architect of victory in the Franco-Prussian war. Moltke was also the creator of the General Staff idea; and showed that it was of no use having courageous, well-armed and well-trained troops unless they could be transported, supplied, fed and brought into action in the most effective and rapid way, supported by adequate reserves, and used according to a proper plan of campaign. All this, of course, has been an accepted part of modern military thinking for the past half century. In 1903–4 when the Elgin, Esher and Norfolk Commissions sat it was something that required to be put into action. But the re-thinking was going deep. The reformers were agreed on one thing—that Britain must go into the next war with a properly mobilized force, equipped, supplied and ready for the field, and supported in the rear by adequate reinforcements.

As Mr. R. B. (later Lord) Haldane remarked when he was facing the task of carrying through the reforms, a mobilisation had to be complete to the last detail. The placing of even one brigade properly supplied, supported and acting on a plan, would be preferable to a host of individual and unconnected units, doled out piecemeal with no proper base staff work and no plan of action. The actual work of Haldane is dealt with in another chapter, for we must now review what happened, in argument, planning and action, in the three years which elapsed between the end of the South African War and his appointment as War Minister at the end of 1906. In 1903 there were many opinions as to the best method of bringing the Army up to maximum strength and maintaining that strength by adequate recruiting methods, and contention raged round the proposal to have a conscripted army on the same lines, if not on the same numerical scale, as those on the Continent. The support for outright conscription was not great. More favour was shown towards a scheme, sponsored by Lord Roberts and other military leaders, for compulsory training for home defence. But both groups were unpopular. Public opinion, as always, was against compulsion of any kind; the newspapers were mainly on the side of the public; and any government which had chosen to go against the stream on this issue would have committed political suicide. There was, too, another and powerful argument against compulsion—the need for economy on military expenditure.

The first steps towards Army reform had been taken during the winter of 1900–1 when G. St. John Brodrick, who had succeeded Lord Lansdowne at the War Office, worked out a plan to re-organise the Army into six commands based on six geographical divisions of the country. Nothing came of this, and real progress was made only after publication of the report of the Elgin Commission which, in the winter of 1903–4 under the chairmanship of Lord Elgin, a former Viceroy of India, sat for fifty-five days enquiring into the conduct of the South African war. A great many unpleasant facts came to light, and it was not surprising that the report, published in the following August, should contain much that was condemnatory. But it was also constructive and proposed, as an insurance against future disasters through inefficiency and unpreparedness, the formation of a War Office Board on the lines of the Admiralty. References were also made to the future constitution of the armed forces and the report leaned considerably towards some kind of national military service so that the army reserves could be properly maintained and the defence of the Kingdom assured. It was perhaps a prophetic instinct that made the Commissioners sign off with these words: "Only an extraordinary combination of fortunate circumstances . . . saved the Empire during the early months of 1900; and there is no reason to expect a repetition of such fortune if, as appears probable, the next national emergency finds us still discussing our preparations."

By this time Hugh Arnold-Forster had succeeded Brodrick as War Secretary and was destined to be in office for three years and do much towards reorganising the War Office and army administration. One of his first acts was to appoint a three-man Commission consisting of Lord Esher (who had sat on the Elgin Commission), Admiral Sir John (later Lord) Fisher, and Sir George Sydenham Clarke (later Lord Sydenham). Exactly a month after their first meeting the Commissioners reported on February 1st, 1904, and as a result the Army Council came into being and the Army had what it had long required—a machine which in peacetime would prepare for war and in wartime would plan and co-ordinate the efforts of the field forces.

The Elgin and Esher Commissions between them had achieved the reorganisation of military administration and had gone a long way towards repairing the deficiencies that had been so glaringly obvious in the recent war. But one big problem remained. How was Britain, short of adopting conscription on the Continental pattern, to ensure the existence and maintenance of a front line force backed by adequate reserves and an efficient means of home defence? The task of finding the right answer was entrusted to yet another Commission under the chairmanship of the Duke of Norfolk, which was to enquire into and report on the state of the Auxiliary Forces. At this time both politicians and militarists were divided among themselves on two inter-related problems— the value of the Militia and the Volunteers as integral parts of the military power; and the wisdom of introducing some compulsory form of enlistment and training. That part-time soldiers put on full-time could play a noble part had been demonstrated in South Africa, but months of dilly-dallying had passed before the Volunteers and the Imperial Yeomanry had become thoroughly prepared for the part they were to play, and any repetition of that, in a modern war against a modern and mobile army would probably prove fatal.

The Norfolk report, published in October 1904, was in favour of universal training for national defence and made specific proposals for the reorganisation of the Volunteers as a force integrated with and matching up to the standards of the Regular Army. Since any invasion of Britain would be made by a large, well-armed and well-trained enemy army, the Commissioners argued that the Volunteers, who existed only for the purpose of meeting and resisting an invasion, must also be well armed and well trained on the same lines as the men of the Regular Army. It was therefore recommended that the new Volunteer Force be organised in Brigades and Divisions, that finance should be wholly in the hands of the Government and that the War Office should supply and supervise all ancillary services and training facilities.

In the meantime there had been a great deal of campaigning up and down the country by protagonists of national service, including Lord Roberts and Lord Milner, who had been in South Africa during the War as High Commissioner. The National Service League had been formed in 1901 with the object of forcing the adoption of some form of compulsory training for all citizens under twenty-five able to bear arms. Some members of the League wanted the scheme applied to the Regular Army; others were in favour of compulsion only for home defence. In January 1906 Lord Roberts, no longer Commander-in-Chief (the office having been abandoned after formation of the Army Council) became President of the N.S.L., which was by this time committed only to compulsion for home defence; and the great soldier threw himself energetically into the campaign by speeches in various parts of the country and fervid championship of the cause in the House of Lords. But even on the limited front of national service for home defence Lord Roberts and his supporters were fighting a losing battle. Their twin enemies were tradition and finance. The overwhelming Liberal victory at the polls in November 1905 meant the reign of a Ministry pledged to economy in the fighting services, and well aware of the large body of public opinion against compulsion of any kind. The reconstruction of the Government following this major election triumph brought to the War Office an energetic Minister, Mr. Haldane, who was to be the constructor of a plan which solved simultaneously the problem of cost and the problem of security. He was not the architect, for he built on the ideas of his predecessors and on the recommendations of the various Commissions. But he built well.

It seems ridiculous in these days, when remembering the astronomical expenditure on arms in two world wars and in the intervening period of so-called peace, to recall that Campbell-Bannerman's Government was against a plan to compel all young men to train for a set period, because even to give four months' training would cost the country one and a quarter million. A microscopic sum, judged by modern standards, but it represented approximately a five-per-cent increase in the Army Estimates. Those who supported compulsion for defence could argue with great common sense that Britain could be invaded by a Continental army if the Royal Navy failed in its task of protection; and that therefore the existence of a well-trained Regular Army was not sufficient unless supported by a well-trained Reserve raised by National Service. But they argued in vain. It was predictable that, in an age when men's minds were turning more and more towards democracy and radicalism, a Government pledged to liberalism and economy in non-social directions should seek a less expensive solution. So Haldane was free to plan in his own way and his Territorial Force was the answer. It was indeed fortunate that an adequate alternative to compulsory service had been found. If the Government of the day had shelved all schemes for strengthening the Army and putting the volunteer movement on a proper basis 1914 might have found us even more unprepared than we were for the onslaught of total war. But by 1914, thanks to Haldane and his advisers, who included Major-General Douglas (afterwards Earl) Haig, an adequate number of Britons in civilian employment had been trained in the use of arms. The Territorial Force in peacetime had proved to be a worthwhile successor to the old Volunteers. And in the first few months of the Great War it was to save Europe.

16

IT has already been pointed out that Haldane's task had been simplified by the findings of the three Commissions, the institution of the Army Council and the General Staff, the expression of public opinion on the question of compulsion, and the Government attitude towards expenditure on the Services. With the construction of the new Regular Army well in hand he was able to concentrate on the Auxiliaries, and he rapidly reached a decision that a completely new structure was preferable to any attempt to graft on to the old Volunteer Force. His opinion of the existing Volunteers was already well known, since some time before he had described the organisation as "probably the most confused thing we have in the British constitution". There was no supply organisation for war and the financial arrangements were hopelessly unsatisfactory. The Volunteer Force as it stood had been condemned by eminent soldiers as "useless for the purpose of modern military necessities". One of the factors which made reorganisation so vital was that recruitment for the Regular Army had gone into a decline. Men were not coming forward in sufficient numbers to make good the wastages of the Boer War and the subsequent retirement of time-served Regulars. The latter circumstance led, of course, to a satisfactory build-up of the Regular Reserve, but there was a grave shortage of men to fill the drafts for garrison duty abroad, and a pressing need for a fighting reserve from which line regiments could be replenished.

The nation had begun the year 1907 with a new Regular Army unable, through a shortage of officers and reservists, to meet its establishment of 6,494 officers and 160,200 men. At the same time the old Volunteers, also below establishment, numbered 241,708 of all ranks and including all services. But numbers alone were not enough. The volunteer artillery were training with out-of-date guns and therefore would have been of little use, without further training, if they had been called upon to operate modern artillery. The infantry training was also rather haphazard; and in general it was clear that a great deal of enthusiasm and devotion to duty was being wasted for want of a proper training programme, up-to-date equipment, well-organised staffwork and adequate ancillary services. It was consideration of all these facts that led Haldane and his advisers to jettison any idea of reforming the Volunteer Force as such. The alternative was an entirely new force based on modern ideas and following as closely as possible the pattern of the Regular Army. And the answer was—the Territorial Force.

The most important difference between the old and the new, therefore, was that whereas the Volunteers until 1900 had never been regarded as part of the Regular Army, the Territorial Force was planned from the start to be constituted, trained and regarded as capable, if the need arose, of going into action alongside, and virtually indistinguishable from, the front-line troops. The main features of the change were the employment of regular officers at divisional and brigade level, staff work controlled by the War Office, complete and efficient courses of instruction, and the use of modern arms and transport. This, of course, was not achieved immediately. And there were not wanting those who scorned the whole idea and regarded Haldane's reforms as impossible of achievement. But history proved Haldane right. Another of his innovations that yielded fruit was the formation of O.T.C. units at public schools and universities. It is important to remember that the scheme for the Territorial Force, although covered by its own legislation—the Territorial and Reserve Forces Act—was an integral part of the general scheme for mobilization in the event of war. So before considering the Territorial Force in detail we must look at the General Plan as visualised by Haldane and his advisers.

1. *The General Staff*

The idea of a General Staff on the lines of that created by

Moltke had been put forward by Brodrick during his brief period at the War Office; included by Arnold-Forster in his own plan, which had been killed by the dissolution of Parliament in 1905; and finally used by Haldane as the foundation of his reorganisation scheme. The General Staff was to function in peacetime on a wartime basis. This, in the general view, was the only way to ensure maximum efficiency in mobilization.

2. *The Expeditionary Force*

With the question of base organisation settled, attention went next to the composition of the forces to be controlled. These, in the Haldane plan, were an Expeditionary Force consisting of front-line troops and reserves and a Territorial Force of volunteers for home defence. The Expeditionary Force in its concise, concentrated form was to be composed of six infantry divisions and six brigades of cavalry, together with all necessary service units, engineers and artillery, manned entirely by fully trained, fit and disciplined men, equipped with the most modern weapons and supplied by adequate services, ready to be transported anywhere at the greatest possible speed so as to arrive at the scene of action in the shortest time and ready to deliver the most powerful blow. In the background was organised the Special Reserve, comprising men in the General Reserve and any who might volunteer from the Territorial ranks for active service with the Regulars.

3. *The Territorial Force*

This was visualised as a force of non-professional soldiers recruited from the civilian population and trained as far as possible to Regular Army standards with these wartime objects:

To supply garrisons for vital points.

To resist enemy invasion attempts.

To expand the Expeditionary Force by voluntary enlistment for service abroad.

The perfect co-ordination necessary to the exercise was achieved by organising the Territorial Force into fourteen infantry divisions and fourteen mounted brigades corresponding to the fourteen military districts into which the country was divided. Each infantry division, commanded by a Regular major-general, was comprised of three infantry brigades with artillery and other auxiliary forces. The Mounted Brigades, each of which was allocated to an infantry division, consisted of Yeomanry, Horse Artillery and other appropriate services. This system kept alive the county and district spirit which had been so useful a feature of the volunteer movement; and did much to dissipate the indignation and regret expressed by old volunteer hands at the passing of the old order.

The Militia, so far as its name was concerned, had no place in the new structure. It had in fact become the Special Reserve, and as such was now part of the Expeditionary Force. The Territorial Force provided the second-line troops, and took the place of the Militia, although organised on a purely voluntary basis.

Each infantry regiment had five battalions. The first two were regular battalions, No. 1 being the first-line battalion and No. 2 a garrison battalion to reinforce No. 2 in the field if necessary. No. 3 battalion was composed of Special Reservists with the task of providing drafts to replace casualties in the two service battalions. The 4th and 5th battalions were composed of Territorials.

An Army Council Order of March 18th, 1908, established a Territorial Force of 11,895 officers and 302,199 men. The Regular Army had been re-established three months earlier at 6,494 officers and 160,200 men, so when the Terriers were in full training Britain would have a total manpower strength, on paper, of nearly half a million. This was regarded as a complete fighting force adequate for emergency, for the Army Council mobilization plan envisaged a complete involvement of the Territorials in time of crisis. The sequence of events in such circumstances would be:

1. Regular Battalions mobilized.
2. Reserves called up.
3. Territorial Force mustered.

It was inevitable that the new force, supplanting a Volunteer movement which had been in existence for half a century, should be regarded with mixed feelings. Haldane had done his best to preserve the old local patriotic spirit by forming county associations, and this move had the effect of mollifying the attitude of provincial landowners and businessmen who had hitherto been most enthusiastic in their support, and who had done so much towards furnishing volunteers and yeomanry for service in South Africa. But there had been a fundamental change, and not even the identification of the Territorials with the county regiments could gloss over the fact. In the vigorous days of the Militia and the Volunteers the Lords-Lieutenant had been powerful and influential, and the county gentlemen had identified themselves willingly and enthusiastically with the local organisations. It is true that in most cases the Lord-Lieutenant became president of the Territorial Association of his county, but there was no escaping the truth that the Force was now an Army organisation, controlled by the War Office, commanded down to Brigade level and sometimes even lower by regular officers; and subjected to rules and regulations emanating, not from the Town Hall or the castle, but from an office in Whitehall. The fundamental change, of course, was that whereas previous governments had viewed the volunteers with detachment and tended to keep them short of help and encouragement, the present régime was intent on doing everything possible (although with a wary eye on the cost) to make the Haldane plan work. This could only be achieved by constructing the organisation within prescribed limits and so discouraging the free-and-easy circumstances in which most of the Volunteer units had operated. The new conditions were accepted by the majority, but there was no consolation for those Volunteer officers and men who were cold-shouldered by the age limit. Many enthusiastic and capable individuals, who would have been willing and able to serve, found there was no room for them at all because they were over thirty-eight. No doubt this represented in the beginning a loss of experience and continuity, but there were two considerations which outlawed sentiment in this matter. The Territorial Force was designed to be fully integrated into the Regulars, operate as a home defence force and provide a reserve of trained men who might supply front-line material in time of war; and therefore it must consist only of men physically capable of undertaking all the duties involved. The other consideration was that since the training would be the same as that of the Regular Army, it was understandable that officers and men over age and therefore not likely to assimilate or take kindly to the new drills and techniques which they would have to pass on to recruits should not be part of a modern force based on up-to-date ideas.

The decision was arbitrary and, like all arbitrary decisions, defective. It deprived the new organisation of men who would no doubt have been able to adjust their ideas and given valuable service, particularly in the early transitional days. But it also cut away a lot of dead wood, and for that reason must be justified as a wise and inevitable decision.

So it was the end of the Volunteers. Almost 150 years had gone by since William Pitt had forced his Volunteer Act through a reluctant Parliament. It was now April 1908. The first Territorial battalions were forming and the first drill halls being planned. A new generation of part-time soldiers was on the stage. The time for "playing at soldiers", if it ever existed, was past. This was the real thing—soldiering with a purpose. The time of trial lay six years ahead, the crucibles of war were still cold, but everyone concerned with the Territorials felt in his bones that he had a tangible object. He was being encouraged to make himself efficient. He was drilled and trained by the latest Army methods. He learned how to operate the newest and most exciting equipment. He was part of the county regiment—in the same "crowd" as the Regulars—and a new pride came into his heart. It stemmed from the same source as had the pride of the Volunteers but was intensified by the fact that he now "belonged", in every sense, to the Regular Army.

In the face of considerable opposition from public, Press and critics inside and outside Parliament Haldane had carried through a reform which was to save Britain from disaster in the World War to come. The seed had been sown earlier, but Haldane and his team had brought to vigorous growth a plant destined to prove fruitful beyond all expectations. It was with justifiable pride that the King, welcoming the advent of the Territorial Force in October 1907, had said: "Henceforth my Yeomanry and Volunteers are to form the Territorial Force—the Imperial Army of the Second Line, which lies within the shores of this Kingdom."

17

I N the last chapter we traced the events leading to the reorganisation of the volunteer movement, the integration of the Territorial Force with the Regular Army, and the development of the theory of the "Expeditionary Force" and the "Second Line". Nearly seven years were to elapse before the theory could be put into practice, and those years were not wasted; yet in reviewing the period immediately following the outbreak of the 1914–18 War it is impossible to resist the feeling that, although Britain was superficially better prepared for a major war than at any previous time, many things had been left to chance for want of practical experience. The chaos of recruiting which followed Government appeals for volunteers was due entirely to the fact that no one in authority had anticipated the magnitude of the response to the call to arms, or had any conception of the wastage of manpower which would occur. No one could be blamed for lack of foresight because the cruel, criminal, senseless butchery of the Great War, experienced by all the European nations involved, was a nightmare of reality which the most vivid and distorted imagination could not have pictured.

Britain was faced with an unprecedented situation. We had an Expeditionary Force which, although the largest ever sent abroad, was pitifully small in comparison with the huge armies of France, Germany and Russia, and was indeed regarded as "a contemptible little army" by the Kaiser. That epithet was to be adopted with pride by the men who had stood in the way of enemy hordes and destroyed German hopes of a quick victory by denying them that

Above, officers of the Imperial Yeomanry at Harrismith in 1900. In the centre of the front row is Major-General Sir H. N. L. Rundle, Commander 8th Division South African Field Frontier Force; *below*, the Army Motor Reserve, reviewed in 1906 at the Staff College, Camberley

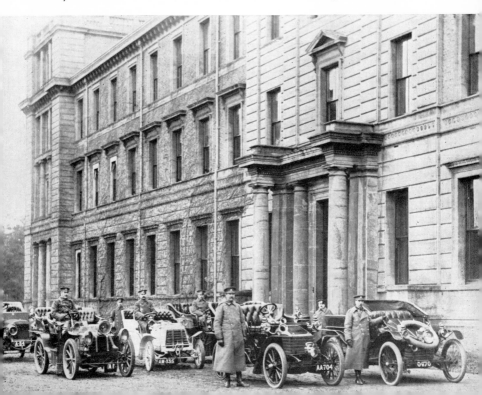

Above, the London Scottish Volunteer Corps, seen here parading at Wellington Barracks, were the first Territorial Infantry Unit to go abroad in 1914; *below*, 1914 volunteers with recruiting-sergeant

occupation of the Channel ports which might well have achieved the object. But it was nevertheless a little army at the start, and proved adequate for the task only because the Second Line was ready for its supporting role—a role from which it was rapidly promoted to share the centre of the stage.

As soon as the mobilization of the Regular Army had been ordered, preparations were made for the embodiment of the Territorial Force, and T.F. units were very quickly in action after the declaration of war—more quickly, in fact, than was strictly proper according to the Territorial and Reserve Forces Act. But that was a peacetime measure; we were now at war, and policy must give place to exigency. The first Territorial Force unit to go abroad were the Oxfordshire Yeomanry, one of fifty-three Yeomanry regiments mobilized, and they co-operated with the Royal Naval Division in the defence of Antwerp. The honour of being the first Territorial Infantry unit to cross the Channel belongs to the London Scottish, and for this reason, as well as its great battle record, its distinctive dress and its peculiarly demo-cratic constitution, this great corps represents all that is best in the Territorial Army.

The genealogical tree of the London Scottish had its roots in the 18th century—if by the term London Scottish one infers a band of London Scots volunteering for military service. In 1798, at the time of the first Napoleonic invasion scare, the Highland Society of London formed the Highland Armed Association, which, shortly afterwards, became the Royal Highland Volun-teers. This corps was involved in the general disbandment of the Volunteer Corps on the signing of the Peace of Amiens; but when the new Boney scare developed in 1803 the past members joined with other London Scots to form the Loyal North Britons, under the command of Lord Reay who two years later handed over the command to the Duke of Sussex. This unit was disbanded in 1814 but when the Volunteer movement was revived in 1859 the Caledonian Society of London, with the help of the Highland Society of London, again pioneered the formation of a unit of London Scots. Dr. Halley, a prime mover in the affair, approached Lord Elcho (afterwards Earl of Wemyss), who was a noted supporter of military affairs in general and volunteer movements in particular. He agreed to join in the enterprise and accept command of the proposed new corps.

Lord Elcho took the chair at a meeting on July 4th, 1859, at which it was decided to form a corps under the title of "London Scottish Rifle Volunteers". A year later the corps was known officially as the 15th Battn. Middlesex Regt. (London Scottish) and in 1880 it became the 7th Battn. During the Boer War some London Scottish members joined the City Imperial Volunteers as individuals, but others combined to form a company of the Gordon Highlanders and went to South Africa with the 2nd Battn. of that Regiment.

In 1908, under the new Territorial Act, the London Scottish became the 14th Battn. County of London Regiment, and paraded as such on June 19th, 1909, when Edward VII presented 108 T.F. units with their first colours at Windsor Castle. But the change in title was really the only change so far as the established Territorial units were concerned. The London Scottish remained the London Scottish and retained all its traditions, including the right to wear the "Hodden grey" kilt and uniform and the Glengarry cap.

When war started in 1914 the War Office planned to send the best of the Territorial units to France in support of the Expeditionary Force, and on September 13th Colonel Malcolm, C.O. of the 1st Battn. London Scottish, was ordered to march his men to Watford and entrain for Southampton, en route for Havre. This decision to give the London Scottish the distinction of being the first T.F. infantry unit abroad drew a congratulatory message from Lord Esher, chairman of the Force. The Territorial and Reserve Forces Act allowed units to volunteer for overseas service in any emergency, but had stipulated that no unit would go abroad until after six months' training. The 1st Battn. London Scottish were in France just one month after starting war training.

Other units rapidly followed suit, and by December 2,413 officers and 66,806 men of the T.F. were serving in Flanders. So far as the Expeditionary Force and the Second Line was concerned the mobilization was effective. But there was no visible plan for handling, equipping, training and accommodating the enormous army which was to follow. In 1899 the Government of the day had been content, unwisely as it proved, to rely entirely on the available regular and reserve forces; and when further recruitment became necessary the organisation for the extra forces had to be constructed. In 1914 the Government of the day, learning part of the lesson of 1899, issued an immediate call to arms; but no real effort was made to regulate the response or ensure that those who answered would be used in the most efficient manner and in the quickest possible time. The appeal, it would seem, was better organised than the preparations for dealing with the response. Within days thousands of men of all ages and from all walks of life had packed their bags, said goodbye to their families, friends and fiancées, bade farewell to their factories, shops and offices, and departed for strange destinations and grim destinies. These men, some of them no longer young and many of them mere boys, had had no training whatever, not even the preliminary training of a Terrier. They were raw recruits from all walks of life, answering the call of King and Country. What no one knew was that they were just a beginning—the vanguard of a mighty flood of manpower which was to flow backwards and forwards on the Western Front during four long, weary and wasteful years.

Recruitment was so haphazard and disorganised that many men both under and over age got into khaki, were sent across the Channel short of training and equipment, were drafted into units for which they had not volunteered, and into jobs for which they were most unsuited. These factors contributed as much as the mistakes of generals and politicians to the waste of manpower in battle; but another serious defect of the chaotic recruiting system of 1914 was the non-selective character of the organisation. Men were taken at face value and allowed to leave important industrial and commercial jobs to join up. They left the mines, the ship-yards, the engineering works and other occupations important to the war effort and the national economy. No one in 1914 could tell them that they would be doing more for the country by stay-ing at their jobs, producing the food, the machines, the guns, the ships and the coal which were to be just as vital to the war effort as the ability to fire a rifle and sustain the physical and mental strain of trench warfare.

Another tragic result of the lack of planning was that good officer material was shamefully wasted. Lord Haldane, as the final part of his reorganisation scheme, had instituted the Officers' Training Corps, and for six years thousands of senior schoolboys and University undergraduates had gone through a course of training specifically designed to qualify them for taking commissions in time of war. It would be idle to pretend that more than a reasonable proportion of these would have proved suitable for commissions when the time came for testing them; but there is no doubt that the chaotic recruiting conditions, the lack of examination facilities, the stranglehold of red tape and the eagerness of recruits anxious to get on with the job led to great numbers of potential officers being drafted into the ranks. They went to France and other theatres of war. They fought gallantly and died nobly. But much better use could have been made of them, and the Army more efficiently and more abundantly officered than it was, if they had been given the commissions for which their preliminary training had fitted them; or at least the chance to obtain them.

In 1939, of course, the war effort was organised and the use of manpower from the start was keyed to the nation's needs. But in 1914 no one had ever thought of "priorities", "reserved occupations" and "age groups". It was a period of patriotic fervour mixed with public hysteria. The lessons had still to be learned and as a result manpower was misused in every possible way. There can be no doubt that, in the crisis caused by the knowledge that we had been plunged into a European War, hasty decisions regarding manpower were made without due consideration of the requirements and with scant preparation for the reception and disposal of recruits. Men under age were recruited by the thousand, many of them only just out of school. A great number of men over age were also taken in, not a few of them grand-fathers. The recruiting-sergeants and officers were actuated by only one object—to get as many fish as possible into the net. At this distance of time it would not be easy to believe all the stories told fifty years ago were they not corroborated at the present day by the veterans who went through these experiences.

Many who should have been rejected at both ends of the age scale were actuated by sincere patriotism or blind enthusiasm—in the young an inspired conviction that they must fight for all they held dear; in the middle-aged a compulsion to do something for the old country. Countless examples of both could be quoted. One "greybeard", born September, 1866, only 5 ft. 2 in. and with no military experience, was accepted for the infantry on his unsupported word that his age was thirty-eight; despite the fact that he later had to produce his marriage certificate, dated 1885, to claim his "separation" allowance. The contradiction in dates was entirely ignored, the fifty-year-old "rookie" went to France and served for some time in the trenches before being given a "base" job. Another man born in 1865 joined up at Birkenhead in 1914, was accepted as thirty-six on his own statement, served for more than two years in the trenches and rose to the rank of Captain.

At the other end of the age scale let us consider a boy barely fifteen who joined the infantry passing as nineteen, then the minimum age, and lost two fingers in France before he was sixteen. He was but one of many who were fledglings at the start of the war but grown, disillusioned men at the end of it; unless, indeed, they had given up their lives while still in their 'teens. One who lived to tell the tale is F. Brutten Cardew of Cheltenham, who presented himself at Exeter Barracks in the uniform of the St. Edward's School (Oxford) O.T.C., gave his age as eighteen (really sixteen) and soon afterwards received the King's Commission in the 3rd Devon Regiment as from August 15th, 1914.

Pure patriotism could account for much of this. But far more potent factors, in the first flush of war enthusiasm, were the example of others, the artful publicity campaigns; and, by no means least, the wiles of the recruiting-sergeant. This individual had not changed a great deal from his counterpart of Victorian or Hanoverian days. He wore khaki instead of a resplendent red uniform, but he had a rosette to indicate his calling, a persuasive line of talk, a cynical disregard for human feelings—and the knowledge that every fish that swam into his net meant a shilling in his pocket. Recruiting officers were equally keen for prestige reasons to snap up as much material as possible, quantity being considered more important than quality. So the impressionable youth, already conditioned by personal feelings of patriotism, pride, and emulation, confronted by recruiting posters and waylaid by the ubiquitous sergeant, was fair game. The process was accelerated by the recruiting march, a feature of recruiting in 1914–15 which will never be repeated. It was, of course, the 20th-century version of the "drum beating" by which recruiters of the last century were accustomed to draw attention to their operations in town square and village market place. I have been permitted to examine documents from the archives of Monmouth Castle, including the following communication, hand-written on blue official paper, and sent on June 3rd, 1875, to the O.C. Royal Monmouth Militia:

"In compliance with paras 1 and 2, clause 16 of the Auxiliary and Reserve Forces regulations of May 12th, 1875, I herewith forward two Beating Orders for Sergeants Harris and Quarman of the Corps under your command, giving them permission to enlist recruits."

Enlistment in those days was achieved by beat of drum followed by "sales talk" by experienced cajolers who knew how to lay it on thick and whose success in getting recruits was in inverse ratio to the I.Q. of their audiences. Since the recruiting sergeant received a shilling for every recruit who signed he had a vested interest in making military service sound attractive. The practice of paying recruiters a *per capita* fee—in more recent times it became half a crown—lasted until 1938, when it gave place to the much fairer method of giving extra pay for this work. Under the bob-a-nob system recruiting sergeants in populous places were naturally much better off than those in country districts.

From drum-beating and colourful exhortations to yokels the science of recruiting eventually developed into the recruiting marches and meetings of the Great War. But the technique was not greatly changed. Still the martial sounds (now, of course, a proper military band) and still the professional "pluggers", perhaps with more polished manners and a more sophisticated line of talk. The procession behind the band would consist of a number of uniformed soldiers marching in military style followed by a few of the smarter rookies in civvies doing their best to emulate the old sweats in front. Stops would be made at likely spots where speeches would be followed by calls to sign on. And during the march itself recruiters would be busy on the sidewalks button-holing likely candidates for the King's shilling. As the war went on a new technique was developed. Soldiers home on leave or slightly wounded would be sent round offices in the big cities, interviewing the clerks in search of likely volunteers.

It might have been thought that there was a tacit understanding among recruiting-officers, recruiting-sergeants, enlistment clerks and doctors that as many men as possible must be enrolled irrespective of age, size, physical condition, and suitability. But in fact everyone concerned, including the recruits, were victims of the system—or, to be more accurate, the lack of a system. As I have already stated, the speed with which the appeal for volunteers was made was not complemented by speed in organising their reception, accommodation, welfare and distribution. For example, one of the biggest reception centres in London was established in Horse Guards Parade in the form of half-a-dozen large marquees, where doctors sat at tables examining applicants. Frequently the rush would be too much for the resident medicos, and temporary reinforcements would be sought from Charing Cross hospital. But house surgeons tackling military "medicals" with no knowledge of service requirements, and anxious to get back to their proper work, could not be expected to deal with the situation in any but a perfunctory manner. This state of affairs, arising from a combination of overworked doctors, enthusiastic officers and eager recruiters, was common all over the country. No wonder, then, that so many men under age, physically unfit, or myopic, were rushed into khaki, later to become victims of their own shortcomings or charges on the country when they broke down in training.

Men now grandfathers who were involved in this chaotic jumble of insufficiency and inefficiency can recall incidents which were all in keeping with the Alice in Wonderland nightmare of a nation going to war and learning the rules on the way. One young man was operated on for a hammer-toe and accepted. Another went for his medical with others to a near-by doctor's surgery, failed to read the letters on the eyesight chart but did so with the aid of the doctor's glasses. The doctor wrote him a prescription, told him to get some pince-nez, carry them on a cord round his neck and put them on his nose *when he had the order to fire.* And I have no doubt the story of how the 63rd Infantry Brigade (61st Div.) reached establishment at Leighton Buzzard was not untypical. Two trains from the North arrived one day to disgorge an amazing assortment of suits, flannels, dungarees, caps, bowlers, straw hats, paper parcels and bags. Most of this motley crew had started from Northumberland and Durham in some sort of order, but on the slow journey South they had themselves "recruited", at various stops, a number of others also eager to answer the mysterious call to duty. They had no nominal roll and there was nobody in charge. "You see that tall fellow in the blue suit", said the prospective C.O. of this heterogeneous band to the subaltern who constituted the other half of the reception committee. "Yes, sir," replied the officer fresh from his school O.T.C. "Very well then," commanded the Brigadier-General, "go and make him a sergeant." It may well be imagined with what painful efforts and through what frustrating situations this Brigade and many others progressed to a state of fighting efficiency, with shortages and delays in equipment and arms, lack of proper accommodation for the winter months, training with dummy rifles, and a general lack of proper guidance from above. But the job was done, and perhaps in no other country in the world could it have been done in such circumstances.

The whole affair seemed to be callous and inhuman, but the individuals responsible for it were themselves powerless to do any more than carry through recruitment in the best possible way and somehow struggle through to efficiency. The individual recruit, naturally, believed that all the things which happened to him were deliberately planned to make him miserable, that all officers were contemptuous of his feelings and all sergeants sadistic bullies.

But many of the things calling for individual complaint were the outcome of policy. It might seem strange to a young man in Northumberland to be taken two hundred miles by train to begin his service; or a lad in Manchester to find himself under canvas in Surrey or sleeping in a barrack square at Aldershot because there was no other resting place for him. But there is no doubt that many a recruit encamped within a few miles of his home would have been much more likely to feel disillusioned than one taken the length of the country away from the old folks. Another common cause of complaint was the cynical disregard for expressed preferences as to units. There were thousands of cases of men opting for particular regiments who, having signed, were sent off for unknown destinations and found themselves enlisted in entirely different units. A mixed collection of recruits, collected from various parts of Surrey, stood in some sort of order on a parade ground at Aldershot and were inspected in contemptuous silence by a sergeant-major who eventually barked that they belonged to the East Surrey Regiment. Immediately there were cries of protest from men who had volunteered for various units not remotely connected with the county. And the reaction of the sergeant-major was predictable: "It doesn't matter what you bloody well joined. You all belong to the East Surreys."

This was typical of a time of urgency in not only obtaining recruits but also preparing them for battle. The situation was rendered still more difficult by a shortage of trained instructors, shortage of suitable accommodation, shortage of training facilities, shortages of arms and ammunition. Everything was in short supply, in fact, except flesh and blood to be turned into cannon fodder as soon as possible and fed to the enemy guns. Lord Kitchener in calling for his new Army had no sentiment about Territorials, and although a great deal of recruiting was done through the T.F., he made it quite clear that he wanted men "for the duration" and for service overseas. Commanding Officers and recruiting-sergeants were told to concentrate on enlisting men for "Imperial Defence" only, and although men were accepted who would not sign to go overseas it made little difference in the end. Each new complete battalion had about 90 per cent Imperial

Service volunteers, and the 10 per cent were more or less obliged to toe the line.

So thousands of raw recruits from town and village, from factory and farm, from university chambers and slumland doss-houses, were drawn into the net. They were sent by train to parts distant from their homes, were met at their destination stations by hardened N.C.O's, drafted into squads, put through a period of intensive training and turned over to their units in ten weeks fit for battle. Or at least fit to be thrust into the hungry jaws of war.

18

ONE prominent feature of the call to arms was the tendency for men of the same calling, nationality, taste and social standing to endeavour to serve together. The Artists's Rifles, the Sportsmen's Battalion, the U.P.S., the Footballers' Battalion, provided notable examples; but these and the many "Pals" units were merely evidence of a British trait which had lasted for centuries. Remember the Devil's Own, formed by London lawyers and thus christened by King George III. At about the same time the Loyal London Volunteers included several groups of this kind which later became famous Volunteer battalions with official designations. In 1798 the clerks of Somerset House formed two companies, and fifty-one years later, following the issue of the War Office Circular, London civil servants formed a corps which became the 15th (City of London) Battalion the London Regiment (Prince of Wales Own Civil Service Rifles). The Civil Service has always been a source of literary talent and Victorian members of the C.S.R. included Anthony Trollope, Edmund Yates, W. S. Gilbert and Charles Kingsley, who served as Chaplain. In 1914 officialdom took advantage of this pleasant tendency, and one notable example was provided by the formation of the 10th (Stk.) Battalion of the Royal Fusiliers, which was filled to overflowing within four days in August 1914 by City workers drawn from the Stock Exchange, the Baltic Exchange, Lloyds and the Banks and Insurance offices. It all began when Lord Kitchener, two weeks after war had broken out, began to plan his New Army. He consulted Major-General Sir Henry Rawlinson,

Bart., then Director of Recruiting but afterwards Commander of the 4th Army, with the result that the following letter was written to Major the Hon. R. White at the Travellers' Club, Pall Mall.

War Office,
Whitehall, August 17th, 1914.

My dear White,

Lord Kitchener is anxious to get a further supply of recruits for the London Regiment, the Royal Fusiliers.

I understand that there are many City employees who would be willing to enlist if they were assured that they would serve with their friends, and I suggest that you collect names and addresses of those who would be willing to serve in the Service Battalion of the Royal Fusiliers in Kitchener's New Army.

The Battalion—which would be composed entirely of City employees—would require a few months' training before they would be fit to serve on the Continent of Europe, but it is the intention of the Military Authorities to send the New Army abroad as soon as it has attained a sufficient standard of efficiency.

Yours sincerely,

H. Rawlinson, Director of Recruiting.

Major White lost no time. Recruiting began in the City on the day after this letter was received, and the first day yielded 210 enlistments. By the following Monday, August 24th, the total had reached 900, by the end of Tuesday the Battalion was well over strength, and by the Thursday, just a week after recruiting had started, there were 1,600 men on the roll. On Saturday, August 29th, 1,147 of these were inspected by Lord Roberts in Temple Gardens, and marched to the Tower of London, where they were sworn in by the Lord Mayor, Sir W. Vansittart Bowater, who afterwards became their Honorary Colonel. Here is Lord Roberts's encouraging address, culled from the records by F. C. Shuter of Northwood, one of the original members of the Battalion:

"Brother Soldiers! I am proud to be the first the welcome you as brother soldiers, and to congratulate you on the splendid example you are setting to your fellow-countrymen, coming forward, as you have done, to take your places in the ranks as private soldiers, not seeking—as a vast majority of men in your station of life are seeking—to be given commissions as officers. We require hundreds of thousands of soldiers, and of these only a minimum number can be officers. Moreover it is absolutely essential that officers should be trained and disciplined—sufficiently trained and disciplined to warrant their being entrusted to command and lead soldiers in war. You are the pick of the nation, highly educated, businessmen, men of various professions, and you are doing exactly what all able-bodied men in the kingdom should do, no matter what their rank or what their station in life may be. I respect and honour you more than I can say. My feeling towards you is one of intense admiration. How very different is your action from that of the men who can still go on with their cricket and football, as if the very existence of the country were not at stake. This is not a time to play games, wholesome as they are in times of piping peace. We are engaged in a life-and-death struggle, and you are showing your determination to do your duty as soldiers and, by all means in your power, to bring this war—a war forced on us by an ambitious and unscrupulous nation —to a successful result. God bless and watch over you all."

After preliminary training at Colchester and on Salisbury Plain the Battalion embarked for France on July 30th, 1915, under the command of Major White, as a unit of the 37th Divn. B.E.F., and served continuously until the end of the war, with more than forty battle honours. The original battalion suffered severely in the first Battle of the Somme on July 13th–15th, 1916, and its total casualties for the war were 742 officers and men killed, died of wounds, or missing; and 1,958 wounded. On August 29th, 1964, a fiftieth anniversary and reunion service in the Tower of London Moat was attended by 104 Old Comrades.

The Royal Fusiliers also had a great accession of strength and quality from a source which many people thought should have been channelled into a more specialised field. This was the University and Public Schools Brigade, started by a Committee of Old Boys and University men with the same idea as that which inspired the Stock Battalion already mentioned. The U.P.S. Brigade had no connection with any University or Public Schools O.T.C., although naturally many of those who volunteered for service had been members of such units. The formation of the U.P.S. Brigade started on Kitchener's Call to Arms and the first poster was ambitious and inspiring in its language:

UNIVERSITY AND PUBLIC SCHOOLS BRIGADE

5,000 MEN AT ONCE

The Old Public School and University Men's Committee makes an urgent appeal to their fellow Public School and University men to at once enlist in these battalions, thus upholding the glorious traditions of their Public Schools and Universities

TERMS OF SERVICE
Age on enlistment 19 to 35, ex-soldiers up to 45 and certain ex non-commissioned officers up to 50 Height 5 ft. 3 ins. and upwards. Chest 34 ins. at least. Must be medically fit.

GENERAL SERVICE FOR THE WAR
Men enlisting for the duration of the war will be discharged with all convenient speed at the conclusion of the War

PAY AT ARMY RATES
and all married men or widowers with children will be accepted and will draw separation allowances under Army conditions

HOW TO JOIN
Men wishing to join should apply at once, personally, to the Public Schools and University Force, 66 Victoria Street, Westminster, London, S.W. or the nearest recruiting office of this Force
GOD SAVE THE KING!

The response was immediate and considerable, and the Brigade eventually consisted of the 18th, 19th, 20th and 21st battalions of the Royal Fusiliers. It was formed not as an O.T.C. but as a Brigade of Kitchener's New Army, and although many members did eventually take commissions the formation went to France as a Brigade towards the end of 1915.

Part of the success of the U.P.S. Brigade recruiting was due—unfortunately so in the opinion of many people—to the laggardly arrangements for deploying the officer material which the O.T.C. movement was presumed to have produced. It was perhaps going too far to suggest, as many did, that a large percentage of recruits who had had O.T.C. experience could have been given commissions automatically. Even the best of them had had no practical experience of war or even of training under war conditions, and could have had only a limited amount of experience in the art of commanding and leading men in the routine business of soldiering. Nevertheless, there must have been a great amount of potentially good officer material in the O.T.C. which was not used, simply because the machinery for employing it was non-existent, or at any rate non-operative, during the first two of three months of the war.

Lord Roberts, as we have seen, was contemptuous of recruits who went for commissions instead of going into the ranks and winning promotion by merit. On the other hand there were many O.T.C. men who felt that the formation of the U.P.S. in itself defeated the object of the O.T.C., and that most if not all of the U.P.S. personnel should have been absorbed by the Officers' Training Battalions formed by O.T.C. officers and other interested persons. The O.T.B.s did eventually provide a good supply of officer material, but not until thousands of potential leaders had been flung into the Western Front battles as Other Ranks when the Army was desperately short of officers. Another contributory cause of this misuse of manpower was the existence of special battalions, including those already mentioned as formed by men of particular callings or interests. There were many men in the ranks of the long-established corps like the H.A.C. and the London Scottish, and many more among the members of the various "Pals" and similar battalions, who refused invitations to train as officers because they did not wish to be separated by rank distinctions from friends who were colleagues in business and comrades in khaki.

The rush to volunteer during the first few weeks might not have been so great if those concerned had not shared the general belief that the war would be short. "It'll be all over by Christmas", the phrase used in the first public reactions to Kruger's declaration of war, had changed to "It'll be all over in four months", and the two ideas had their common birth in optimistic wishful thinking. Far-sighted and experienced men felt otherwise, and Kitchener's uncompromising appeal to young men to enlist "for three years or the duration" was, as it transpired, no pessimistic reading of the situation. The fact that the establishment of Kitchener's first 100,000 took much longer than had been expected was in itself an indication of how enthusiasm had cooled. White-hot patriotism was the driving force behind the streams of young men crowding into the recruiting centres in the last days of that 1914 summer. But the future was mercifully hidden in those early days and so the men and the boys and the greybeards rallied to the call of King and Country. They came from the mines, the shipyards, the factories, the technical establishments; creating a supply of fighting power so large that it far extended the capacity of the existing organisation to deal with it, and at the same time taking hands which could ill be spared from lathes, rivetting guns and test tubes.

This chaotic misuse of manpower was to have serious consequences, since so many of the Western Front casualties were caused by failures to maintain the supply and quality of munitions. Many thousands must have been killed or wounded in war because of shortages of material caused by their very absence from their machines and benches.

One of the problems associated with the tremendously high wastage of manpower in the Western Front battles was the difficulty of sparing combatant troops for home defence purposes. The answer was an appeal to over-age and medically unfit men to volunteer for duties connected with the safety of public service

Above, First World War volunteers take the Oath and, *below*, are kitted out

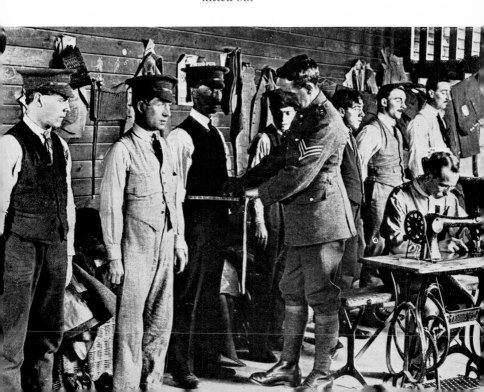

Above, a column of volunteers—the 20th Battalion London County—marching through Chislehurst, Kent, on their way to barracks; *below*, Home Guards of the Second World War on manœuvres

installations and other vital points in danger from threatened enemy action or the activities of saboteurs.

Railway stations, waterworks, gasworks and power stations were among the obvious places requiring supervision, and the Volunteer Corps was formed for this purpose. The members, including a large proportion of grand-dads, wore grey uniforms and armlets, and spent many night hours, unarmed, patrolling sites and buildings which might be the objectives of anyone seeking to pollute our water supplies or wreck essential services. The Railway companies formed their own national guards detachments for similar purposes, and the whole effort was not unlike the Civil Defence movement of the Second World War.

A great deal too much, in the early days of the war, was left to individual impulse and the independent policies of employers. While many firms in the big cities readily acquiesced in their younger employees enlisting, in many cases paying full or part salaries to those who had dependents; there were many instances of employers, for commercial reasons or in the public interest, imposing their own checks on indiscriminate enlistment. The Government also had areas of control, foreshadowing the complete organisation of 1939, when the Schedule of Reserved Occupations combined with conscription effectively reduced the number of spontaneous volunteers. The Postmaster-General, for example, issued an order forbidding established Post Office employees to enlist, and until this ban was lifted on September 8th, 1914 in favour of a system of controlled permission anyone joining the Forces was considered to have resigned his appointment and forfeited all benefits. The reason for the ban during the first six weeks of the war was that when Regular Reservists and men of the Supplementary Reserve had left their jobs, together with those called for service with their T.F. units, the Post Office faced a serious manpower problem which, if unchecked, could have crippled the country's communications. When the ban was lifted most Post Office employees joined the Post Office Rifles, the P.O. Royal Engineers or the Signal Corps or worked in Army post offices.

Eventually a more coherent system of official control of

recruitment developed, but not before there had been serious inter-
ference with the war effort of industry. And long before then the
first wave of enthusiasm had spent itself. One has only to read
some of the war books, both autobiographical and fictional,
which sprang from the 1914–18 war, to realise how the first
expressions of patriotic fervour gave way, under the burden of
events, the effects of official incompetence and neglect, and the
sheer misery of life in overcrowded barracks and inclement
training camps, to a sullen doggedness of spirit from which all
the glamour had departed. Thousands of young men went into
the war longing to come to grips with the Germans for the sake
of patriotism and all its represented. Thousands of them died
without even seeing a German soldier in action. And long before
they died, that winter of training in 1914–18, with its mud and
ill-fitting clothing and shortage of arms and all the other defects of
a situation that had got out of hand, had sapped everything from
them except the will to go on and "finish it".

19

IN March 1916 Britain, for the first time, introduced conscription for service overseas. Three factors contributed to this step. The early enthusiasm for volunteering had subsided; the war had already lasted far longer than anyone had expected; and the wastage of manpower made it impossible to maintain the supply by voluntary enlistment. So we had first the Derby scheme and then total conscription, and the days of free-and-easy volunteering had gone for good. But by this time the Territorial Force had become indistinguishable from the Regular Army. The Terriers had fought side by side with the Regulars in many great and bloody battles, they had suffered terrible casualties, won many honours, and had proved on countless occasions that the faith of Haldane and those who fostered the development of the peacetime Territorial Force had not been misplaced. Nevertheless, it was impossible to envisage a return, after the war, to the Territorial Force as it had been before 1914. The war had taught us many things, and one of the lessons was that the conception of a Second Line as purely for home defence was no longer valid. For some time after the end of the war, however, questions of this kind had only an academic value. In the general reaction after the Armistice problems of war and defence were very far from the public mind. Demobilization, house-hunting, work-finding, the building of a land fit for heroes, whether the Kaiser should hang, how much Germany should pay—these were the pressing problems of the day, and they took precedence over any idea of preparing for the next war. Besides, there wasn't going to be a next war. President Wilson and the League of Nations would see to that. So the men of the Territorial Force were demobilized along with their Regular comrades and in 1920 the Force itself stood down. Not for the first time in our history the end of the emergency was followed by official disinterest in the voluntary movement. But something had to be done to effect post-war reconstruction of the national forces, and in 1922 the Terriers were reconstituted under a new title—The Territorial Army. The change was significant. It represented one more step in the integration of volunteers and regulars, and the conditions of enlistment obliged recruits to the new T.A. to sign to serve overseas if required.

Twelve years passed by, during which the T.A. found its feet, recruited in a leisurely manner, and did little more than maintain the county associations and organise the drills and summer camps on a peacetime basis. Then, in the mid-thirties, the situation began to change. Various events—the unprovoked Japanese aggression in Manchuria, the rise of Adolf Hitler in Germany, the trumpetings of Mussolini in Italy and the palpable failure of the League of Nations to control its members, had turned men's thoughts to the risk of another world war. There were powerful movements for peace at any price, even at the cost of condoning aggression and accepting acquisition. But Governments could not afford to rely on pious slogans and fond illusions that the peace-loving masses would prevail over their war-minded rulers. The demonstrations in Trafalgar Square echoed dismally in Whitehall, where the problem of manpower in the Services was becoming acute. This was due partly to the fact that Britain had played a leading role in the abortive disarmament talks and therefore had to set an example in reduction; and partly to the unpopularity of the Army. Enlistment was again on a voluntary basis, but one big war in which conscription had been found necessary had wrought a great change in the public attitude towards Army life. At the end of the 19th century the distinction between the officer class and the rank and file was clearly marked. The most that any private in the Regular Army of 1899 could hope for in promotion was to become a warrant officer; and commissions could be obtained only by those whose social standing was acceptable and who could afford the expense involved. In the Boer War many young men of the latter category fought in the ranks alongside Tommy Atkins, and the class barrier was breached. It was broken down completely in the Great War, when thousands of men were given commissions from the ranks and many reached positions of high command.

The old order of things was not entirely washed away in the post-war era. The young man who fancied an Army career could still go through the traditional avenues of Woolwich and Sandhurst, but if these avenues were closed to him for financial, social or scholastic reasons he could join the ranks in the knowledge that there was no rung of the ladder unreachable by determined feet. Unfortunately the Army itself had not kept pace with this change in emphasis. A stage had been reached when it was necessary to attract good material, but the pay, conditions of service and accommodation all compared unfavourably with civil life, and even the unemployed, of whom there were many in those years of depression, hesitated to sign for the Regular Army and so remove themselves for several years from the labour market. For these and other reasons the Regular Army, so far from being up to establishment (210,000 in April 1936) was well below strength and the recruiting rate was so poor that it could not even keep pace with the annual wastage. The actual strength at that time was just over 197,000, but a year later, although the establishment had been increased to 221,000, the numbers had fallen to 193,700, or roughly 12 per cent below par. The Regular Army was in the doldrums, but the plight of the Territorial Army was worse, since in the economic situation of the country the available resources had to be applied to the task of keeping the first-line troops efficient and well equipped. So the Terriers were not only below strength in numbers but possessed no auxiliary or ancillary services, suffered from a reduction in training grants, and had to be content with mainly out-of-date and sub-standard arms and equipment. The total strength of the Territorial Army in April 1936 was 129,700, or about 28 per cent below establishment, and the tendency, as in the Regular Army, was for the numbers to fall.

In 1937 the international situation forced government action to increase the size and efficiency of the Services. A combination of circumstances, including an official advertising campaign and a growing realisation among the people that another world war was possible, led to rapid improvement. Within a year the Regular Army reached establishment, and the Territorial recruiting also showed a welcome increase. Then came "Munich" in September 1938. The public might have been lulled by wishful thinking into a sense of security by Chamberlain's "peace in our time" message, but everyone in authority was well aware that the only vital product of the Prime Minister's meeting with Hitler was a breathing space which must be utilised to the utmost. In January 1939 the Government made two important decisions. They created a Directorship of Mobilization and issued a Schedule of Reserved Occupations. Although the Director of Mobilization was appointed by the War Office and the Schedule drawn up by the Ministry of Labour the two were inter-related, their main object being to make the best possible use of available manpower and so avoid the haphazard enlistment of 1914 which, as illustrated in the previous chapter, had the effect of crippling industries which were of vital importance to the war effort. Two months later Mr. Leslie Hore-Belisha, the War Minister, opened a campaign for doubling the Territorial Army. It was a large-scale operation, mounted with a cunning appreciation of human nature. There had been a general call to the nation to volunteer for one of the many services, with the emphasis on civil defence and fire fighting for men and women who could not join the Services, and on the Territorial Army for young men. Commercial and industrial firms were encouraged to sponsor recruiting by their younger employees, and in many cases platoons and even companies were raised consisting entirely of workmates. Official encouragement and the growing possibility of war stimulated recruiting at such a rate that by August 1939 the Territorial Army mustered 428,000 men as against 204,000 in the previous January.

Typical of this response is the story of how the London Scottish met the challenge to every T.A. unit to double its size. Lt.-Colonel Duncan Bennett, addressing the 1st Battalion on April

3rd, explained the Government policy, which involved, at the outset, the transfer of 119 officers and men to the resuscitated 2nd Battalion. As soon as these plans were made public there was a rush of London Scots to join, and many old members of the regiment were also in the crowds which besieged their Headquarters in Buckingham Gate. Thanks to a lot of round-the-clock work by the resident staff, the medical officers and the Old Comrades, the rush was controlled and absorbed efficiently. By April 21st, less than a month after the Government announcement, 630 men had been enrolled; and the Regiment was congratulated by the Secretary for War on being the first in the country to complete duplication. And the start of a waiting list was evidence enough that the regiment was living up to the watchwords suggested by Lord Elcho on its formation—"Discipline, Efficiency, Permanency". This doubling of strength so quickly was in keeping with the regimental record. When the Territorial Force was formed in 1908 the London Scottish were the first of the London Regiment Battalions to reach establishment; and, as has already been related, they were the first T.A. infantry battalion to go to France in 1914.

So the Territorial Army was more than doubled within nine months. Meanwhile the Military Training Act had been passed on May 26th. This was historic, for never before had Britain had compulsory enlistment in time of peace. All men on reaching the age of twenty were obliged by the Act to do six months' service in the Royal Navy, the Army or the Royal Air Force, followed by three and a half years in the Reserve with a liability to undergo annual training. The Military Training Act was short-lived, being superseded by the National Service Act which was passed on the day war was declared. As a result only one intake of Militiamen, amounting to 35,000, was made under the Military Training Act, but the few months in which it had been in force had enabled machinery to be set up which was used for the purpose of organising wartime conscription. On September 3rd, 1939, therefore, the land forces of the country consisted of a Regular Army of 224,000, Reservists to the number of 28,000 who had been recalled to the Colours, another 74,000 Reservists of varying degrees of efficiency according to how many years they had spent in the Reserve; about 42,000 in the Supplementary Reserve, 35,000 Militiamen taken in under the Military Training Act, and a Territorial Army of 428,000. On paper, the Terriers outnumbered the Regular and Reserve forces, but in actual fighting strength were well under 400,000, because about 40,000 men were found to be medically unfit or too young for overseas service, and in the first three months of the war nearly 12,000 others had to be returned to industry because they were affected by the Schedule of Reserved Occupations. This schedule had not been applied to the T.A. in peacetime because it was believed important to do nothing which might affect the response to the Territorial recruiting campaign. But the decision to permit indiscriminate enlistment of Territorials created considerable mobilization and training troubles when war began. It was not only that a significant percentage of individuals had to doff khaki and resume their working clothes, but also that the disappearance overnight of complete units, such as an anti-aircraft battery of miners and an infantry company formed from the workers of one shipyard, caused complications which were not easily ironed out.

But the hard, well-trained core of the Territorial Army was already proving itself. Various locally-recruited coastal defence units were scattered around our shores. Five divisions of A/A units were also organised on a local basis. The remainder formed the mass of the T.A. in nine infantry divisions, three motorized divisions and two brigades of mounted cavalry, with standards of drill and equipment indistinguishable from those of the Regular Army. Three of these divisions went to France as part of the Expeditionary Force, while the remainder manned the home defences and, of course, did yeoman service in the Battle of Britain. From 1939 onwards there was no difference save in name between the two Armies. As in 1914, the integrating effect of war was complete.

The success of the campaign to double the Territorial Army was due partly to an announcement by Leslie Hore-Belisha that any man not older than twenty who became a Territorial would be exempt from the provisions of the Military Training Act. This was calculated to appeal to the characteristic British dislike of conscription and resulted in a considerable intake of teenagers who preferred to sign on for four years as Territorials, with periodical drills and training camps, rather than spend six months in the Services and three and a half in the Reserves. Many of those who came forward were found to be too young and others not of the required standard of fitness when the war actually started, but the great majority were retained. The upper age limit was applied to discourage enlistment by men who might be affected by the Schedule of Reserved Occupations. Nevertheless, the Territorial Army attracted many men over twenty-one who, realising that in the event of war there would be conscription, preferred to be volunteers.

There was naturally less enthusiasm for the idea of joining the Regular Army, which involved full-time service in peace, and the recruits to the Colours in the twelve months following Munich were mainly young and starry-eyed romantics who wanted adventure. One, self-confessed, of this kind is L. McIntosh of Snodland, Kent, who, feeling certain that war was inevitable and wanting "action", decided in November 1938 to join the Guards. After passing the literacy test and a preliminary medical examination at the Coldstream Guards' recruiting office he was sent with others to Caterham Barracks, where a weeding-out process, including a full "medical", resulted in several of his fellow-recruits being sent home, some of them under age. One of the recruits was a deserter from a Scottish regiment, who, after escaping detection for three weeks, gave himself away by the soldierly smartness of his kit! The raw recruits were used in company with seasoned soldiers in recruiting marches round London and other big cities, but the image of martial pump and valorous deeds soon gave place to the hard reality of Army life. Some recruits had to wait a long time for uniforms and the supply of modern arms did not keep pace with the increase in manpower. The war was several months old before some members of the new army were made acquainted with any weapon more complicated than the rifle. It was impossible for the thoughtful ones among these volunteers to avoid the impression that some official thinking, at any rate, was on 1914–18 lines.

The pattern, indeed, was being repeated. We went into the South African War with the Crimean image of riflemen in squares repelling attacks or advancing in line with fixed bayonets, and found to our dismay and discomfiture and that Boer did not fight that way. Having discovered the value of cavalry in South Africa we went into the 1914–18 war very cavalry-minded, but quickly got bogged down in trench warfare. In 1939–40 we and our Allies, with trench warfare in mind, relied on defensive positions and the Germans made it a war of movement, circumventing the Maginot Line with their armour.

It might be thought that, with the campaign for Regular Army recruiting running alongside that for the Territorial Army, and the existence of the Military Training Act, there would be no scope for spontaneous volunteering on the actual outbreak of war, as there had been in 1914. Obviously there could be no repetition in scale of that great rush to join up, no 1939 version of the First Hundred Thousand, no equivalent of Kitchener's Army. But there was a surprisingly large amount of voluntary enlistment on September 3rd, 1939, and for some weeks afterwards. Queues of men formed outside the principal recruiting offices and many men signed on, although some of them had their papers cancelled when it was found they were in reserved occupations. A love of adventure no doubt inspired many to anticipate the operations of the National Service Act, and there were, as usual, individuals who wanted to change from dull jobs or sought Service life as a solution to domestic or personal problems. But one important reason for this enthusiasm was the belief that, by volunteering, one would be able to choose one's unit. Before the days of compulsion Army regulations made it impossible for a man who enlisted for a particular unit to be directed to another, and many would-be recruits in peacetime, unable to join a selected regiment, were lost to the Army altogether. The Military Training Act and its successor changed all that. Any man who was directed would have to do his service in the unit chosen for him, thus enabling the recruiting organisation to maintain an even flow of recruits into the various regiments and branches of the Service. Many young men forestalled this arbitrary situation by volunteering in advance of direction. The Royal Air Force was popular but very selective. The Navy, too, could afford to look out for the most suitable material. But the Army with its wide non-specialist field offered jobs for everyone, and the Army recruiting offices were kept busy during those weeks of September and October 1939. Then, gradually, the National Service Act took full effect. Men were called up by age groups according to their occupations, and for the first time Britain was fighting a major war with its total man-power under the control of the State. The National Service (Armed Forces) Act, to give it its full title, extended liability for military service to all men between eighteen and forty-one. At the same time the Territorial Army was officially merged with the Regular Army.

20

IT has been necessary so far to concentrate attention on the development of Britain's military power as it applied to the volunteer movement. Now a further reference to the volunteer movement in naval circles is required, and appropriate consideration must also be given to volunteers of the air, products of the 20th century who played such heroic and distinguished parts in World War II.

There were valid reasons why the Senior Service should be so far behind the military arm in acquiring true volunteer attachments; and a very obvious reason why the air arm should be last on the scene in that respect. Nevertheless, it must be recalled that the Royal Naval Volunteer Reserve and its Royal Marine counterpart ante-dated the Territorial Army by four years, this being due principally to the compelling urgency of a situation caused by the great progress of Germany towards competition with Great Britain in naval power. I have already explained (see Chapter XVI) how the general opinion in high naval circles in the latter part of the 19th century was in favour of the Royal Naval Reserve, composed of time-served professional sailors, to the almost total exclusion of civilian volunteers. The R.N.R. represented in the official view the only really efficient reserve, being composed of men who had had experience of service afloat with the Royal Navy and who, being liable to recall in emergency, could easily be drafted to ships or shore stations in the knowledge that they would require a minimum of re-training to fit them for the jobs. In Admiralty circles, in consequence, there was a disposition to regard any body of civilians partially trained under peacetime conditions as a liability rather than an asset. It is possible that the formation of the R.N.V.R. and the R.M.R. would have been delayed considerably, and perhaps the history of the early days of the Great War altered to the Allies' disadvantage, if the country had still been slumbering in the cosy contentment of the nineties.

One hundred years earlier, as we have seen, the general surge of military volunteering in face of the Napoleonic threat had its nautical counterpart in the formation of the Coastal Fencibles. Fifty years later the construction of a new force of land volunteers was paralleled by the institution of the Royal Naval Coast Volunteers. And after the lapse of another half-century, the situation called for a new conception of the parts which civilians might play, in both Services, to ensure adequate defence of the country and support for forces serving abroad. The military side of this development progressed at the slower tempo, for reasons already stated, and it was so early as 1903, after many arguments in high places and desperate rearguard actions by naval chiefs echoing the prejudices of their predecessors, that the formation of the Royal Naval Volunteer Reserve and the Royal Marine Volunteers was authorised by Parliament. All was by no means "ship-shape and Bristol fashion" with the new organisations for several years. As in the case of the military volunteers in earlier days, the part-time civilian sailors had need of all their unquenchable enthusiasm to carry them through many disheartening circumstances caused by official indifference and parsimony. Fortunately they did carry on, and the onset of the First World War saw the R.N.V.R. and the R.M.R. ready for instant action alongside the Territorials. The only difference was that whereas the Territorials went to war in their battalions, the great majority of the nautical volunteers were formed into brigades designed primarily for land fighting. And it was in land fighting, first in the defence of Antwerp which helped to delay and frustrate the enemy plans for occupying Channel ports; and later with such renown and great sacrifice on the beaches of Gallipoli, that most of them saw action.

One of the reasons for the formation of the Royal Naval

Division, apart from expediency, was a long-standing prejudice against employing volunteer sailors in responsible sea-going roles. This prejudice had its roots far back in the 19th century, and was crystallised in the report of the Tryon Committee in 1890, which recommended the disbandment of the Royal Naval Artillery Volunteers as having little or no value for genuine naval purposes. This was a little hard on a bunch of keen types who, being obliged to limit their training to the use of light artillery and small arms, and being officially designated for the defence of coasts and ports, had for years been only too willing to take advantage of the very occasional chances they were given of training afloat.

On the outbreak of the 1914–18 war very few R.N.V.R. personnel found their way into ships. But as the war went on so the value of R.N.V.R. training was made apparent, and a force which, in August 1914, had numbered fewer than 5,000 officers and men, had increased eight-fold by the time of the Armistice.

It required a major war to convince diehard naval regulars that civilian reservists were essential to a well-conducted and properly-constituted Navy, and in 1921 the R.N.V.R. was reconstructed in such a fashion that, in all aspects, its members could become indistinguishable from R.N. personnel in actual service. In 1937 the R.N.V. Supplementary Reserve was formed from amateur sailors and merchant marine officers, and there is no doubt whatever that all that was done in these directions in the 1930's had a distinct and vital effect on the national effort in World War II. When mobilisation was ordered towards the end of August 1939 nearly 10,000 officers and men, representing the combined strength of the R.N.V.R. and the Supplementary Reserve, with their various ancillaries, were called to their posts and responded with alacrity and enthusiasm. The trained peacetime reservists were rapidly assimilated into the fighting Navy, many going straight into responsible posts, while the volunteers from the untrained civilian ranks were coming forward to opt for the Senior Service.

From September 1939 onwards all recruits for the Naval services became R.N. for the duration but the peacetime R.N.V.R.

went into the Second World War well equipped to provide officers and responsible senior ratings for duty anywhere.

In the 1914–18 conflict the R.N.V.R. had a limited purpose, but in 1939–45 its duties were diverse in the extreme, carrying out duties in every conceivable type of war vessel from battleships and aircraft carriers down to the "little boats". Mine-sweeping and mine-laying, bomb and mine disposal, submarine hunting, convoy work, commando landings, M.T.B. patrols, sea rescue work, everything came naturally to these men who, although civilians in peacetime, had been trained in the traditions of the Royal Navy and could bear comparison with their R.N. comrades.

And they fought on no narrow front. In the Atlantic and the Pacific, in the various Mediterranean operations, in the Far East and on the Arctic circle route to Russia. Wherever, indeed, any naval activity was in progress. It has been estimated that during World War II R.N.V.R. officers outnumbered regular R.N. officers by at least two to one.

In the natural order of things the volunteer part-time airman was the last to appear in history. He did not materialise, indeed, until that immediate post-war period in the 1920's which saw the reorganisation of the Territorials and the R.N.V.R. The air arm was of course very much a product of the 20th century, and suffered many growing pains owing mainly to public indifference and official scepticism about the value of aviation as a means of waging war. It seems incredible in these jet-propelled and supersonic days that there should ever have been a time when the aeroplane, once developed, should not immediately have been recognised as a war weapon of unlimited possibilities. But other countries as well as Britain tended to disregard aviation as anything more than a hobby for enthusiasts and a sport to be indulged in by those willing to risk broken necks for the sake of excitement. The light was perhaps a little later in dawning for us than for certain other nations, but the outbreak of war in 1914 did not find us entirely unprepared, although still subject to lack of enthusiasm in Government circles. Not unnaturally the early development of war aviation was along military lines, and the service which was to become the Royal Air Force had its genesis in the South African War, during which the Balloon Section of the Royal Engineers was of great assistance in a campaign depending a great deal on accurate observation of furtive enemy movements. Little was heard of this after the Boer War until in 1910 Mr. Haldane, his mind as usual fixed on the probability of a big European War and the necessity for preparation, set aside part of the balloon factory at Farnborough for experiments in the design and construction of aeroplanes. From this small seed, under the impulse of two World wars, sprang the present Royal Aircraft Establishment, which has its shop window in the Farnborough Air Show.

In April 1911 an Air Battalion of the Royal Engineers was formed, commanded by an Army officer, Major Sir Alexander Bannerman, and comprised of one balloon company and one aircraft company. The latter attracted the attention of young and enterprising Army and Navy officers, some of whom had already had some practical experience of "messing about in planes".

As there were at this time not many more than fifty licensed pilots in the land, including civilians, the movement had a modest start, but as knowledge of and interest in flying spread the Air Battalion soon became too small. It was now realised officially, although the idea was resisted by the Army, that aviation for war purposes had to be regarded as a separate arm, and in May, 1913, the Royal Flying Corps was formed, absorbing the Air Battalion and embracing both naval and military pilots. The naval officers concerned quickly knit themselves into an exclusive body, with headquarters on the Isle of Sheppey, where the famous seaplanes and flying-boats of Short Bros. were later to be constructed. These pioneer naval airmen were greatly encouraged by Winston Churchill, then in his first term of office as First Lord of the Admiralty.

It is outside the scope of this book to deal with the pre-war frustrations of the new arm, but it is a matter for interest that whereas the R.F.C. at the start of World War I had 179 aeroplanes of greater or lesser efficiency and 1,244 officers and men, the total air strength of Britain at the armistice totalled 22,647 aircraft and 291,000 officers and men. All these were members of the Royal Air Force which had been formed early in 1918 by the amalgamation of the R.F.C. and the Royal Naval Air Service.

All the volunteers for active flying during the war were of course full-time members of the R.F.C. or the R.N.A.S., and the first part-time volunteers were actually ground operators. In October 1915, under the threat of developing Zeppelin raids, the Observer Corps was formed—a body of men of all classes and occupations who served at night, after a full day's work in office or factory, in isolated units at points along the East and South coasts as well as near London and other big cities. The successors of these pioneers served with the Royal Observer Corps in the Second World War and played a distinguished and important part in the Battle of Britain.

In 1920 the naval authorities, never happy at being incorporated in the R.A.F., had their way and the Fleet Air Arm was formed. Five years later came the big opportunity for many World War I airmen who had returned to their civilian jobs although still young enough to fly. This was the formation of the Auxiliary Air Force, which became an immediate success because it appealed not only to demobilized wartime airmen but also to many younger men who had since ventured into the new element, and who regarded the opportunity for increasing flying experience at the nation's expense as too good to miss. The world of aviation had advanced considerably since 1913-14. Flying in one sense had become commonplace in that no one any longer stared open-mouthed into the sky at the appearance of an aeroplane. But it was still a great experience to be aloft and an even greater thrill to be at the controls and therefore, for a short time at least, master of the air.

So the success of the A.A.F. was predictable. At first it consisted modestly of four squadrons, but by the outbreak of World War II it had developed into an effective striking force which played an important role not only in the Battle of Britain but in many other air operations of the war. Indeed, the first success against enemy aircraft over British territory was gained by the Scottish Squadron of the A.A.F. when enemy bombers flew up the Firth of Forth and returned minus two of their number, shot down by part-timers turned full-timers. Much has been written about the County of London (601) Squadron, formed mainly through the energy and enthusiasm of Lord Edward Grosvenor; and also of the Eagle Squadron, manned by American volunteers. But one must beware of becoming invidious, for many more A.A.F. units played equally distinguished but less publicised parts in the war of the air.

Members of the A.A.F. might be regarded as the first Territorials of the Air, but there were other later volunteers also entitled to be included in that category, for in 1936, in the fact of mounting evidence of Germany's aggressive policies and warlike preparations, the Royal Air Force Volunteer Reserve was formed. The difference between the two corps was that the A.A.F. was composed of volunteers recruited locally from men having flying experience, whereas the R.A.F.V.R. was specifically limited to men of eighteen to twenty-five who were to be trained in flying and ground duties. It was designed to be the principal means of entry into the R.A.F. in wartime and was in fact so used.

21

NATURALLY there were great numbers of men, including old soldiers, who were itching to be part of the Armed Forces but were either over age or in reserved occupations. For these the overrunning of France and the Netherlands by the Germans in the Spring of 1940, and the crisis of Dunkirk, provided the great opportunity.

Every age, as we have seen throughout this history, has had its particular brand of popular feeling, and it would be unwise to seek for parallels. Yet in many ways the remarkable scenes and situations resulting from the volunteer movement of 1803 had its 20th-century counterpart in the birth of the Local Defence Volunteers, and the development of this force under its later and permanent title of Home Guard.

The two situations were almost identical. An enemy was in possession of the French coast at its nearest point to England, and in virtual control of the whole European continent from the Skagerrack to the Pyrenees. An invasion of British shores seemed to be imminent, and the available forces already in service might not be sufficient to withstand an onslaught if it came. But there were two important factors which did not exist in 1803 and accentuated the urgency of the steps to be taken in 1940. We had had our Dunkirk and were involved in a tremendous effort to re-equip and reform our regular forces as a priority task. And of course the menace of airborne invasion was something quite new in the history of these islands, although there had been plenty of examples of its efficacy during the previous two or three years on the Continent. By the time the "phoney war" ended in the German sweep to the Channel coast we had no illusions about the power opposed to us or the potential danger in the enemy's successful invasion techniques—the dropping of parachutists to seize important strategic footholds, and then the flying in of troop carriers with men and arms to consolidate the ground already won.

The situation was explained by Anthony Eden, then Secretary for War, in a broadcast on May 14th. After giving a warning that what has happened in Holland and Belgium might well happen in Britain at any time, he announced the Government's intention to raise a force comprised of men between sixteen and sixty-five not engaged in civil defence of any kind, who were willing to "do their bit" in defence of the country. The new force would be called Local Defence Volunteers and anyone could join by handing in his name at the nearest police station. The words were scarcely out of his mouth before front doors were shutting all over Britain and men converging on the police stations. The rush had started so quickly that, in the absence of special arrangements, there was a delay of some weeks in coping with it.

It is not difficult to understand why Eden's appeal received such a spontaneous widespread response. Although defence was the stated object of the exercise, every man who answered the appeal was captivated by the idea of being on the offensive. The decision to form the L.D.V. provided an opportunity for demonstrating that desire to fight which was latent in the average masculine breast. It appealed strongly to ex-Servicemen—veterans of the Boer War and those who had volunteered during World War I. It also brought a gleam to the eyes of retired Regulars, and pensioned-off sergeant-majors and sergeants were to be the mainstays of many of the local companies formed in towns and villages throughout the land. But the idea appealed no less strongly to thousands who had never used rifle or revolver, and so far as drill was concerned knew not their right hands from their left. To them, as well as to the veterans of other wars, this was a positive way of serving the country. Already many thousands of men and women had deployed themselves on the Home

Front in A.R.P., A.F.S. and other organisations, and they were to
give splendid and self-sacrificing service in the Battle of Britain
and what followed. But all this work was for defensive purposes.
The L.D.V., although enrolled for defence, was offensive in
character. These volunteers carried offensive weapons, in the
beginning of a modest and perhaps not lethal kind, but implying
that the emphasis was to be on doing damage to the enemy, rather
than repairing the damage he was to do to us. It was this thought,
as well as the instinctive desire to do something once the objective
had been indicated, which caused our police stations to be beseiged
on that May evening.

I have already dared to draw a parallel, in the formation of the
L.D.V., to the raising of the great volunteer army in face of the
"Boney" invasion scare of 1803. But there is no true precedent
for the Home Guard, to use its historic name, because it was
recruited literally overnight with the possibility that it might be
in action the following night. The case was as urgent as that. In
1803 those who drilled and learned the use of arms were preparing
for enemy action which could succeed in its object of a landing
only if wind and weather were favourable and if the British Navy
had been rendered powerless. Even then ample warning would
be available and the direction of the attack predictable, allowing
the deployment of forces to meet it in the virtual certainty that
only one area of coastline would be involved. But on that night
of May 14th, 1940 no one could be sure that invasion of a far
different kind was not a matter of hours away; that Hitler's generals, having carried their blitzkreig through to the Channel
coast, might not be planning an immediate strike across the
Strait while we were still reeling from the effects of Dunkirk,
engaged in re-grouping our forces, and still short of the armaments and men required to withstand attack. It was perhaps
obvious to the expert that the enemy also required time to re-
group and consolidate, and to replenish supplies, before proceed-
ing to the next move. But to the ordinary man, now in the street
on his way to the police station, the Eden broadcast meant that
every moment was precious and vital; that even as he wrote his
name in the register, German paratroops might be girding on

their harness and boarding the planes for the "March against England".

A more appropriate allusion to past history might be to the ancient Britons who sprang to arms, grabbing what offensive weapons lay to hand, and made ready to defend their country and their homes against the Romans. The L.D.V.s were to be organised in sections attached to limited localities, but all parts of larger local units which in turn were parts of county units. And in the big cities sections or companies were formed by business firms and factory owners specifically to defend particular premises and the surrounding areas, or to protect vital undertakings and services.

Later that summer, on the suggestion of Sir Winston Churchill, the L.D.V. was renamed the Home Guard. It was also officially incorporated into the Army. Officers of the Home Guard received His Majesty's Commission and the various battalions were attached to Regular regiments, coming under the divisional commanders for the districts and receiving drill and training by the latest methods, and in many cases operating very modern arms and equipment. All this, however, took a long time. In the beginning matters were very far from being perfect. There was never any question that we would get the men. The problem of a uniform was easily settled, for on the day after Mr. Eden's broadcast the War Office announced that volunteers would be issued with denim uniforms and field service caps. Later, when the supply situation improved, they were clothed in khaki serge battledress.

The big problem was the provision of arms. The factories were hard at work making good the losses of Dunkirk. Nothing coming off the supply lines at that time and for some months afterwards could be diverted for the use of the Home Guard, not even rifles. So in the beginning it was a case of "do it yourself". Volunteers turned up with their own weapons—shot guns, old Service revolvers, swords, daggers, clasp knives and many weird and wonderful home-made weapons of offence. Nothing which might be used to kill a paratrooper or knock him senseless was despised, and many of the conversations that ensued in the village halls and country barns, or in the more sophisticated guard-rooms provided in factories and office buildings, became technical discussions on the value of various improvised weapons and the most effective use of bare hands if all else failed.

There were also bright ideas in official quarters, and some not so bright, for tiding over the waiting period. Pick handles were very popular, at least with the officials who thought of supplying them. And there were some rude remarks in Parliament and else-where about one general's suggestion that pikes be issued as standard weapons for the new force. There was no doubt about the plenitude of pick handles, and in at least one Fleet Street news-paper office they could be seen on the shoulders of sub-editors and reporters in denim uniforms patrolling the corridors and the roof-tops at night.

Some of the more enterprising members of this particular Company had coshes slung on their belts. Another wore a dagger, and one tough Australian who had fought at Gallipoli had strapped to his thigh a massive Service revolver. The best cosh, it appeared, was made from a foot length of ribbed garden hose into one end of which had been inserted a few inches of lead piping. The general idea was that if one should come upon an enemy paratrooper on rounding a corner one would dig the pick-handle into his stomach and as he doubled up hit him on the back of the neck with the cosh. There were various guard-room demonstrations, with diagrams of vulnerable parts of the anatomy, and much practice in commando operations, including sneaking up behind an enemy sentry, clapping a hand over his mouth, and sticking a knife into his back between the shoulder blades. It seemed to be assumed that enemy soldiers would remain passive receivers of such treatment, but some London Home Guards very quickly realised that this was an illusion when they attended a course in guerrilla tactics in Osterley Park, home of the Earl of Jersey. The instructors included three Spaniards who had fought in the Spanish civil war. They taught the Home Guards how to lay mines in the road and explode them by remote control from a neighbouring ditch. The Spaniards drove a car towing an old wooden truck as target, and all the Home Guards had to do, having laid the mine in the road and concealed the wires leading to the ditch, was to press the button at the right time. It all seemed a very comfortable way of waging war until, after two or three successful explosions, the car made another pass over a newly laid mine. Before the Home Guards could do anything two of the Spaniards leapt out of the open car straight into the ditch and brandished knives in a very ferocious manner. Those who had that experience never forgot the lesson as, in the months ahead, they went through their exercises among the blitzed buildings of Central London.

Such training was very useful, and no doubt would have been of great value if an enemy invasion had taken place. But during that fateful summer and autumn of 1940 the Home Guard had a different role to play.

Fires raged in the City, there were constant air raid alerts, and many of those on Home Guard duty joined with Air Raid Wardens and the fire services in limiting the damage, rescuing people and valuables, and clearing up the mess. There were no demarcations lines in this war, no "who-does-what" disputes. It was total involvement, and a situation very different from that envisaged by those who had rallied to Anthony Eden's call. But however the character had been changed by circumstances, the Home Guard proved its value, ranged alongside the various civilian organisations on the Home Front. A massive and indomitable line of defence which involved women and even children as well as men, which kept high the morale of the people, and which made a significant contribution to victory.

22

IN 1945 the Territorial Army stood down, and, as on the previous occasion in 1920, this was a prelude to reorganisation. This time there was a big difference. In 1920 conscription automatically ended with the general demobilization. In 1945 the National Service Act remained in force, and when the Territorial Army was reconstructed in 1947 as part and parcel of the Regular Forces of the nation, it could no longer function as a purely voluntary body. With young men still being called up for national service no great accession of voluntary recruits could be expected. Indeed, in the first three years after reconstruction only 80,000 enlistments were from volunteer sources, and this severe under-manning led to National Service men being posted to Territorial units instead of to Regular battalions. The total strength of the T.A. in 1952 was given as 198,500 men, of whom 131,500 were National Service enrolments. A fifty-per-cent expansion was provided for in the 1953-4 estimates and the Territorial Army was now a great, efficient, well-equipped and disciplined force ready to be deployed with the Regular Army in any emergency which might arise. Although the influx of national service men had destroyed the hitherto purely voluntary character of the Territorial Army, the voluntary spirit remained vigorously alive. After all, many of the national service men would no doubt have become Terriers had there been no National Service Act. And most of the rest who could be classed as unwilling conscripts absorbed the ideas of comradeship and mutual support which the Territorials and, indeed the Regulars, had fostered. Another important factor was that the voluntary elements of the Territorial Army provided the leaders; and the true Terriers, young and old, continued to regard their county and local headquarters as places where the fraternal idea of working and playing together still flourished.

While it had been necessary to integrate the Territorials with the Regulars in peace, as they had been and would be in War, the Territorial Army remained a separate institution, partly because the county associations were too valuable to be discarded, partly because the "amateur" atmosphere helped recruiting, and partly because of the necessity for having separate organisations for the purpose of pay, grants and other administrative details. So the T.A. reconstruction, although placing the Terriers under military discipline and military law, with its organisations controlled from Whitehall, retained the county associations, mostly under the presidency of the Lords-Lieutenant as before. There were also county committees composed partly of civilians who were responsible for all peacetime activities and services of the regiments, including the supply of equipment and the provision of drill halls and other accommodation. The money came from grants included in the annual Army Estimates; and some idea of the strength and importance of the modern Territorial Army may be gathered from the fact that, six years after its revival in this special form, the Army Estimates set aside £15,000,000 to cover grants for a force of 300,000 men.

Just a hundred years had passed since the issue of General Peel's famous Circular. In 1859 the Government of the day had given way reluctantly to public opinion without relaxing its parsimonious grip on the purse strings; and had authorised a modest volunteer force consisting mainly of riflemen with no auxiliary services and operating as local groups with no centralised command. In 1959, after three wars in which its worth had been proved over and over again, the volunteer movement had received full recognition. After a few more years had passed the Territorial Army underwent another transformation—regretted by many but believed by the authorities to be the only solution to efficient organisation of the country's manpower. Only time can show whether, in solving that problem, we have killed or at any rate seriously undermined the true volunteering spirit.

It is clear that in the effort to reduce our military structure mainly for reasons of economy there was a tendency to remove all traces of those sixty years of glorious Territorial tradition, and the hardened volunteer who served in the Territorial Force or the Territorial Army—or both—might be pardoned for regarding April 1st, 1967, as an appropriate date for the official inauguration of the Territorial Army Volunteer Reserve. This represented the second reincarnation of Haldane's creation, and only an eleventh-hour decision by the Government preserved some vestige of the old idea. The Territorial Army, even after the reconstruction of 1947 already referred to, was a composite body of men all having the same degree of responsibility, the same conditions of service, the same facilities, the same rewards, and the same freedom. The new T.A.V.R. is composed of three separate organisations, with three distinct roles and different conditions of service and remuneration. The first of these, the T.A.V.R. I has an establishment of 1,600 with the tasks of providing logistic support to any United Nations force which might be formed, and to combine with the "Ever-Readies" to form the Special Army Volunteer Reserve, with the liability to serve for six months when called out, an annual bounty of £150 and an extra £50 on being called up. The "Ever-Readies" form part of T.A.V.R. II which has an establishment of 50,800 and exists to increase the active strength of the Regular Army in the event of operations involving British forces, in circumstances which make the Regulars inadequate for the purpose. Their annual bounty is £60 per man with a payment of £50 on being called up by Royal proclamation. These two sections are classed as Volunteers, practically indistinguishable from the Regular Army, with duties of Regular soldiers, and trained, equipped and armed to the same high standards. To ensure their readiness for action in all circumstances the T.A.V.R. II members will have fifteen days' camp training annually, this being held abroad every third year.

T.A.V.R. III is the only section having an affinity with the old Territorial Army. It is indeed an attenuated version of the

"Terriers", with an establishment of only 23,000 officers and men, entitled to no bounty, with scarcely a foreseeable chance of training in the use of heavy armament or armour, and required to do only eight days in camp each year. Apparently the whole of this third force has a budget of £3,000,000, which suggests that, on the terms outlined and pending any official reconsideration on review, many of these volunteers of the third degree will find it costs them money to be included in Britain's last line of defence. This, of course, has been the lot of volunteers through the ages, and those in authority who gave grudging consent to the formation of T.A.V.R. III might feel that modern warfare demands a close-knit military formation of highly-trained men ready for instant action, rather than a very large body of men required for home defence. For this reason the rôle of T.A.V.R. III has been limited to helping in the maintenance of law and order in the event of internal strife, and co-operating with the Civil Defence authorities in the event of war.

Fortunately this drastic reorganisation of the Territorial Army has not meant the disappearance of the county Associations, and there is no doubt that thousands of Terriers up and down the country will keep alive the great Territorial traditions. Nevertheless it is impossible not to feel dispirited by the present trend, identified as it is with retrenchment on defence expenditure, reduction of British commitments overseas, and a general scaling down of military organisation. The pessimists might say that the "amateur soldier" is no more—that this is the end of the story.

But is it? Will there be another chapter in the history of the Volunteer? Will there be anyone left, after the next War, to write history? More than 150 years have passed since the Younger Pitt said of the Volunteers of 1803 that they had helped to save England by their efforts and Europe by their example. Nearly seventy years have gone since Kipling sang of the absent-minded beggar. And since then we have had two hot wars and a number of cold ones. Who will write the next panegyric on the next effusion of patriotic fervour? Certainly it would be a confession of despair to imagine that the modern concept of war has killed the volunteer spirit. The only change has been in the technical approach to war itself. When an interval of four minutes separates peaceful co-existence from the destruction of civilisation there can be little scope for do-it-yourself heroism and altruism. The next war will be fought by instruments under remote control and the finger that presses the button might well rock the world. One of the many inspiring posters of the First World War showed a typical Tommy lighting his pipe and saying "'Alf a mo, Kaiser." That "'alf a mo" could be too long an interval next time.

But away with pessimism. The history of our nation shows that the hour has almost invariably produced the men, and one must trust posterity to repeat history. It was an English poet laureate who, just over a century ago, helped to inspire the Victorian renaissance of the Volunteer movement. So let one of Scotland's great poets speak of the deathless pride of race which is the mainspring of all national endeavour:

> "Breathes there the man with soul so dead;
> Who never to himself hath said
> This is my own, my native land. . . ."

Appendix I

BIBLIOGRAPHY

Amery, H. S.: *The Times History of the South African War.*

Baker, Harold: *The Territorial Force* (MURRAY, 1909).

Barclay, C. N.: *The London Scottish, 1939–45* (CLOWES, 1952).

Berry, R. P.: *A History of the Volunteer Infantry* (SIMPKIN MARSHALL, 1903).

Biddulph, Genl. Sir Robert: *Lord Cardwell at the War Office* (MURRAY, 1904).

Brett, Maurice E. (Editor): *Journals and Letters of Reginald Viscount Esher* (IVOR NICHOLSON & WATSON, 1934).

Brophy, John: *Britain's Home Guard* (GEO. G. HARRAP & CO., 1945).

Burns, Lt.-Col. A. H.: *The Agincourt War* (EYRE & SPOTTISWOODE, 1956).

Chatterton, E. Keble: *The Auxiliary Patrol.* (SIDGEWICK & JACKSON).

E. P. Cheney: *The Dawn of a New Era* (HARPER, 1936).

Clarendon, Edward Hyde, 1st Earl: *A History of the Rebellion.*

Clode, Charles M.: *The Military Forces of the Crown* (MURRAY, 1869).

Codrington, Col. G. R.: *The Territorial Army* (SIFTON PRAED, 1938).

Cruickshank, C. G.: *Elizabeth's Army* (O.U.P., 1946).

Dudley, D. R. and Webster, G.: *The Rebellion of Boudicca* (ROUTLEDGE AND KEGAN PAUL, 1962).

Dunlop, Col. J. K.: *The Development of the British Army, 1899–1914* (METHUEN, 1938) and *The T.A. Today* (BLACK, 1941).

Esher, Viscount: *Journals and Letters*

Fortescue, Hon. J. W.: *The History of the British Army* (MACMILLAN, 1906).

Fortescue, Sir J.: *Wellington* (WILLIAMS & NORGATE, 1928).

Graves, Charles: *The Home Guard of Britain* (HUTCHINSON, 1943).

Halevy, Eric: *The Rule of Democracy* (ERNEST BENN, 1934).

Harling, Robert: *Amateur Sailor* (CHATTO & WINDUS).

Haverfield, Prof. E.: *The Roman Occupation of Britain* (1924).

Hay, Col. Jackson: *The Constitutional Force.*

Holmes, T. R.: *Ancient Britain* (1907).

Holt, Edgar: *The Boer War* (PUTNAM, 1958).

James, David: *The Life of Lord Roberts* (HOLLIS & CARTER, 1954).

Keeson, Maj. C. A. C. :*History and Records of Q.V. Rifles 1792–1922* (CONSTABLE, 1923).

Lancaster-Woodburne, G. B.: *The Story of our Volunteers* (NEWMAN, 1881).

Lennox-Kerr, J. and Granville, Wilfred: *The R.N.V.R.* (HARRAP, 1957).

Lewis, Michael A.: *History of the British Navy* (O.U.P., N.Y., 1959).

Lindsay, Lt.-Col. J. H.: *The London Scottish in the Great War* (LONDON SCOTTISH H.Q., 1925).

Lloyd, E. M.: *A Review of the History of Infantry* (LONGMANS GREEN, 1908).

Loyn, H. R.: *Anglo-Saxon England and the Norman Conquest* (LONGMANS, 1962).

Macaulay, Thomas Babington, Lord: *History of England.*

Maxwell, Donald and Gordon: *The Motor Launch Patrol* (Dent).

Marriott, Sir J. A. R.: *England Since Waterloo* (METHUEN, 1913).

Maurice, Maj.-Gen. Sir Frederick: *Haldane, 1856–1918* (FABER & FABER, 1937).

Mitchell, R. J. and Leys, M. D. R.: *A History of the English People* (LONGMANS GREEN, 1950),

Nickerson, Hoffman: *The Armed Horde, 1793–1939* (PUTNAMS, N.Y., 1940).

Osman, Sir Charles: *History of War* (METHUEN, 1898) and *Wellington's Army* (LONGMANS GREEN, 1912).

Osmund, J. S.: *Parliament and the Army, 1642–1904* (CAMB. U.P., 1935)·

Peel, Hon. Sidney: *Trooper 8008 I.Y.* (ARNOLD, London 1902).

Plummer, the Revd. C.: *Anglo-Saxon Chronicles.*

Powieke, Sir Maurice: *The Thirteenth Century* (O.U.P., 1953).

Raikes, Capt. G. A.: *The First Regiment of Militia* (BENTLEY, 1876).

Repington, Charles a-Court: *Vestigia* (CONSTABLE, 1919).

Richards, Walter: *His Majesty's Territorial Army* (VIRTUE, 1916).

Roberts, Michael: *The Military Revolution, 1500–1660* (UNIV. OF BELFAST, 1956).

Scobie, Capt. I. H. Mackay: *An Old Highland Fencible Corps* (BLACKMORE, 1914).

Scott, Sir Sibbald David, Bart.: *A History of the British Army* (CASSELL, PETTER & GALPIN, 1880).

Scott, Sir Walter: *The Antiquary.*

Sebag-Montifiore, C.: *History of the Volunteer Forces* (CONSTABLE, 1908).

Sheppard, E. W.: *A Short History of the British Army* (CONSTABLE, 1950).

Stowe, John: *Annales* (1580).

Stubbs, William: *Select Charters* (1870) and *Constitutional History of England* (1873-8).

Thompson, Dr. David: *England in the Nineteenth Century* (PENGUIN 1950).

Treece, Henry and Oakeshott, Ewart: *Fighting Men* (BROCKHAMPTON PRESS, 1963).

Trevelyan, G. M.: *English Social History* (LONGMANS GREEN, 1942).

Tunstall, Brian: *William Pitt, Earl of Chatham* (HODDER & STOUGHTON, 1938).

Verner, Col. Willoughby: *Military Life of H.R.H. George, Duke of Cambridge* (MURRAY, 1905).

Walker, H. Goold: *The Honourable Artillery Company.*

Walter, James: *The Volunteer Force History and Manual* (CLOWES, 1881).

Wedgewood, Cicely V.: *The Common Man in the Great Civil War* (LEICESTER U.P., 1957).

Williamson, J. A.: *The Age of Drake* (BLACK, 1946).

Wrottesley, Lt.-Col. the Hon. George: *Life and Correspondence of Sir John Burgoyne, Bart.* (BENTLEY, 1873).

Young, Brigadier Peter and Adair, John; *Hastings to Culloden* (BELL, 1964).

———

The Soldier's Companion, 1878.

The British Volunteer, 1799.

The T.A.—Any Volunteers?—War Office Pamphlet (C.O.I., 1952).

Committee on Administration of the T.A. (Report) (H.M.S.O., 1955).

Statutes at Large (Ministry of Defence Library—Central and Army).

And Various Regimental Histories (Ministry of Defence Library—Central and Army).

The Reserve Army and National Security, Maj.-Gen. R. F. K. Goldsmith (The Army League, 1966).

Appendix II

STATUTES CONCERNING VOLUNTEERS
AND RELATED SUBJECTS

1181.	The Assize of Arms.
1285.	The Statute of Winchester (Hen. II).
1306.	13 Edward I c 6.
1326.	1 Edward III c 5. (An Act against impressment into service).
1345.	18 Edward III c 7.
1351.	25 Edward III c 8. (Limited the King's powers to impress men without Parliamentary approval).
1403.	4 Henry IV c 13 (confirmed 25 Ed. III c 8 and extended jurisdiction to Wales.)
1404.	5 Henry IV c 3.
1488.	4 Henry VII c 7. (Appointing Yeomen of the Guard and Grooms of the Bedchamber).
1511.	3 Henry VIII c 3 and c 4. (Regulations for practice of Archery and for Service in War Beyond the Sea).
1551.	3/4 Edward VI c 5. (Sanctioned appointment of Lords-Lieutenants to each county or shire).
1557.	4/5 Philip and Mary c 2. (Repealed all previous statutes and established a national force at expense of subjects).
1603.	1 James I c 25. (Revived all statutes repealed by 1557 Act).
1660.	12 Charles II c 15. (Disbanded the Army).
1661.	13 Charles II c 6. (Establishing the King's sole right of control over the Militia).
1662.	14 Charles II c 3. (Establishing City of London Militia).
1663.	15 Charles II c 4. (For the better ordering of the Forces).
1688.	1 William and Mary c 5. (The Mutiny Act).
1690.	2 William and Mary c 12.
1691.	3 William and Mary c 7.
1692.	4 William and Mary c 6.
1694.	5/6 William and Mary c 19.

O

1694.	6/7 William and Mary c 13.
1695.	7/8 William and Mary c 16.
1696.	8/9 William III c 35.
1697.	9 William III c 31.
1698.	10 William III c 18.
1699.	II William III c 14.
1700.	12/13 William III c 8.
1702.	1 Anne c 17 and c 15.
1703.	2/3 Anne c 14.
1704.	3/4 Anne c 15.
1705.	4/5 Anne c 10.
1709.	8 Anne c 13.
1733.	7 George II c 23.
1739.	13 George II c 17. (Exemption of volunteers from impressment).
1743.	17 George II c 15. (Regulations for recruiting).
1744.	18 George II c 7. (Authorising formation of "Associations for Defence").
1745.	19 George II c 2. (Calling out militia).
1756.	29 George II c 35.
1757.	30 George II c 8 and c 25. (The Militia Act, providing for the first time for a Ballot).
1757.	31 George II c 26. (Providing for the enrolment of Volunteers in the Militia).
1759.	33 George II c 2 and c 22.
1779.	19 George III c 76. (Authorising 30,000 Volunteers separate from Militia).
1786.	26 George III c 107. (This Act "for amending and reducing into one Act of Parliament the laws relating to Militia in England" provided for a Ballot, with five years' service from those chosen by ballot, and permission for substitutes. Fine of £10 on evasion. The Act also provided for the acceptance of volunteers for service in the Militia, and empowered the King to embody the Militia "in all cases of actual invasion or upon imminent danger thereof, and in all cases of rebellion or insurrection".
1794.	34 George III c 16. (This Act represented an extension of 26 George III c 107 and contained these important provisions: "Whereas in the present situation of Public Affairs, it is highly necessary and expedient that the

number of the Militia Forces be augmented . . . be it therefore enacted that if any person or persons . . . shall offer to H.M. Lieutenant of any County to raise one or more companies to be added to the Regiment or Battalion of any County or Riding, it shall be lawful to accept such offers . . . and it shall likewise be lawful . . . to accept and cause to be enrolled any number of Volunteers to be added as Privates to the establishment of such Regiments or Battalions". The Act also provided for Volunteers to receive the same bounty as other members of the Militia, and, like them, to receive the same pay as Regular Forces when and if embodied.

1794.   34 George III c 31. (Authorised separate battalions and companies of Volunteers with exemption from Militia Ballot).

1796.   37 George III c 3 and c 22.

1798.   38 George III c 18, c 19 and c 27. (Registering all able-bodied men 15–60 for defence of all kinds).

1799.   39 George III c 106.

1801.   42 George III c 12.

1802.   42 George III c 90 and c 91. (Military Service Act, extending scope of 38 Geo. III c 27).

1804.   44 George III c 56. (The Volunteer Act).

1806.   46 George III c 91.

1807.   47 George III c 71.

1807.   48 George III c 3. (The Local Militia Act which created a new Militia of 60,000 and discouraged enrolment in the Volunteers).

1809.   49 George III c 53.

1811.   51 George III c 20.

1812.   52 George III c 38. (An Act establishing a permanent local Militia by ballot and enabling the Crown to form an Establishment for each county or place on the following basis:
"So long as the number of Volunteers, Yeomanry, etc. in a county amount to six times the original quota of Militia for that county fixed under the General Militia Act, no enrolment to be made; but enrolment to be made to bring up the number to strength".

1813.   53 George III c 81.

1816.   56 George III c 3. (This Act disbanded the Militia Ballot, and was followed by an Order in Council commanding that no ballot or enrolment for the London Militia take place for one year. Similar orders in Council were made annually by the Privy Council up to and including 1936). (See 15/16 Victoria c 50).

1820.   1 George IV c 100.

1852.   15/16 Victoria c 50. (Under this Act the Militia was first raised entirely by voluntary enlistment and continued to be so. Original quota for England and Wales was 80,000 to be increased by another 40,000 in the event of War.

1853.   18/19 Victoria c 57.

1854.   17/18 Victoria c 105, 6 and 7.

1859.   22/23 Victoria c 40. (Authorising establishment of the Royal Naval Reserve).

1863.   26/27 Victoria c 65 and 69. (The Volunteer Act. To consolidate and amend the Acts relating to the Volunteer Forces of Great Britain).

1869.   32/33 Victoria c 81.

1871.   34/35 Victoria c 86. (Act for Regulating the Auxiliary Forces and integrating Volunteer Forces with Regular Army).

1882.   45/56 Victoria c 49. (The Militia Act—To consolidate the Acts relating to the Militia).

1896.   59/60 Victoria c 33.

1897.   60/61 Victoria c 47.

1900.   63/64 Victoria c 39.

1902.   2 Edward VII c 6. (Act relating to the Royal Naval Reserve).

1903.   3 Edward VII c 6. (Act establishing the Royal Naval Volunteer Reserve and the Royal Marine Reserve).

1907.   7 Edward VII c 9. (The Territorial and Reserve Forces Act. To provide for the reorganisation of H.M. Military Forces and for that purpose to authorise the establishment of County Associations for raising and maintaining a Territorial Force; and for amending the Acts relating to the Reserve Forces).

1921.   11/12 George V c 37. (The Territorial Army and Militia Act. To provide for the application of a new designation ("Territorial Army") to the Territorial Force and the

Special Reserve, and to repeal enactments relating to the
Militia and Yeomanry).

1948.   11/12 George VI c 64. (The National Service Act).

1949.   12/13 George VI c 96. (Auxiliary and Reserve Forces).

1950.   14 George VI c 30. (National Service).

1951.   14/15 George VI c 23. (Reserve and Auxiliary Forces).

1953.   1/2 Elizabeth II c 50. (The Auxiliary Forces Act. To consolidate certain enactments and Orders in Council relating to the Territorial Army and Royal AuxiliaryAir
Force and to empower H.M. to maintain the T.A. and
the R.A.A.F.).

1954.   2/3 Elizabeth II c 10. (National Service).

1955.   3/4 Elizabeth II c 11 and c 20. (Revision of Army and Air
Force Acts).

1962.   10/11. Elizabeth II c 10. (National Service and Auxiliary
Forces).

1964.   12/13 Elizabeth II c 11. (National Service and Auxiliary
Forces).

Appendix III

CHRONOLOGY

Date	Event
Date	*Event*
55 B.C.	Julius Caesar lands in Britain.
A.D. 47.	Claudius invades Britain.
61.	Revolt of the Iceni under Boadicea.
189.	Severus invades Britain.
410.	Rome invaded by Goths. Romans withdraw from Britain.
446.	Vortigern invites Angles to help him defeat Picts and Scots. Angles land at Ebbsfleet.
494.	Cerdic the Saxon lands and starts six years' campaign which conquers Wessex.
793.	Norsemen invade Northumberland. Lindisfarne plundered.
835.	Danes invades Sheppey.
851.	Danes stay over winter for first time.
869.	Danes overrun East Anglia.
878.	King Alfred introduces military system—the "fyrd", forerunner of the national militia.
900.	Death of Alfred.
1013.	Sweyn begins brief Danish dynasty in England.
1066.	Battle of Hastings.
1086.	William I introduces the Feudal System.
1145.	Accession of Henry II.
1173.	The Feudal Rebellion.
1181.	The Assize of Arms.
1205.	King John reforms Army service.
1264.	Barons win Battle of Lewes, followed by institution of British Parliament.
1285.	Statute of Winchester (Edward I) ordains that every man under sixty must arm himself at his own expense.
1415.	Henry V invades France (the first excursion of a new "King's Army" differing in many respects from the Feudal Host.)

1459.   Unofficial date for origin of Cheshire Yeomanry (Battle of Blore Heath, Shropshire).

1483.   First mention of "defensible personis" (The Fencibles).

1485.   Henry Tudor lands at Milford Haven. Battle of Bosworth and death of Richard III.

1486 c.   Henry VII establishes "Yeomen of the Guard".

1537.   Henry VIII incorporates The Fraternity of the Guild of St. George, progenitor of the Honourable Artillery Company.

1551.   Lord-Lieutenancy instituted and Lords-Lieutenant take the place of Sheriffs as commanders of Militia in the shires.

1588.   Spanish Armada. London Trained Bands at Tilbury officered by members of the H.A.C.

1595.   Bow as weapon of war abolished by Privy Council. Calivers and muskets issued to H.A.C.

1614.   James I orders general muster of London Militia. (This represented a re-organisation of the Trained Bands, henceforth known as Militia.)

1621.   Earliest known date for formation of Volunteer Corps. Example of "Artillery Company of London" followed in various provincial cities.

1638.   Branch of H.A.C. formed in America by emigrant members of the London Company, under the title of "The Ancient and Honourable Artillery Company of Boston, Mass."

1642.   Civil War establishes Parliamentary Control over the Militia.

1643.   Estates of Scotland summon "all fensible personis within the Kingdom between sixty and sixteen".

1648.   Commissioners of the City of London strengthen the Trained Bands and Auxiliaries and appoint Colonel, Major and five Captains of Horse "for the defence of King, Parliament and the City".

1649.   Council of State authorises "a foote company of Volunteers to be raised in the towns of Birmingham and Aston for the service and safety of the county".

1651.   Governor of Bristol authorised to receive volunteers to serve either separately or with the Militia.

1655.   Cromwell divides England into areas governed by major-generals and backed by a new Militia.

1660.   Charles II introduces first standing army.

1674.   House of Commons ordains that the Militia, the Pensioners and the Yeomen of the Guard are the only lawful armed forces in the realm.

1676. Royal Company of Archers formed in Edinburgh.

1685. Accession of James II. Monmouth's rebellion.

1689. Bill of Rights declares a standing army illegal in time of peace.

1690. Devon invasion scare.

1725. General Wade organises "The Highland Watch" from clans favouring the Hanoverian cause (forerunner of The Black Watch).

1744. France declares war and "The Gentlemen Volunteers of London" formed..

1745. Mayor of Bristol is offered "an association for the defence of the Town and H.M. Government". Glasgow meeting "to raise as many men as can be had to bear arms".

1757. Militia Bill (introduction of the ballot).

1758. Militia Bill amended to allow Militia captains to accept volunteers in place of militiamen compulsorily furnished by each parish.

1759. William Pitt begins reorganisation of the Army and the the Navy. List of officers of Colonel Thornton's Regiment (now 3rd West York) approved by the King. (This was the first regiment to be raised under the Militia Act.) The Government approves scheme of Lord Forbes of Culloden for raising a Fencible Corps in the Highlands.

1763. Peace with France. The Militia disembodied.

1778. American War of Independence. Militia embodied for five years.

1779. Irish allowed to organise a volunteer movement.

1780. Gordon riots. London Trained Bands, Militia and H.A.C. in service.

1789. Sussex Fencible Cavalry formed. Warwickshire Yeomanry formed. New Volunteer movement inspired by Pitt the Younger as Warden of the Cinque Ports.

1792. Militia re-embodied (and served with short breaks till 1814).

1793. Expansion of Fencibles consequent on War with France. Hampshire Carabiniers and Suffolk Yeomanry formed.

1794. Act passed to increase Militia "owing to the state of public affairs". Surrey Yeomanry formed and volunteer "to serve anywhere". London Trained Bands reorganised as "The London Militia".

1795.   Formation of Shropshire Yeomanry. "London Volunteer Cavalry" help the H.A.C. to put down riots.

1796.   Parliament sanctions a Supplementary Militia.

1797.   French landing near Fishguard. Pembroke Yeomanry in action. Militia force raised in Scotland. Mutiny of the Nore (Kent Yeomanry patrol coast).

1799.   Temple Bar and St. Paul's District Volunteers and the Guildhall Volunteers Association amalgamated as "Loyal London Volunteers".

1803.   War with France. Threat of Napoleonic invasion.

1810.   Somersetshire Yeomanry called out to suppress riots in Bath.

1813.   Defeat of Napoleon. Fencibles disbanded.

1814.   Napoleon abdicates. All Volunteer Corps relieved from duty and disbanded. (This order specifically exempted the H.A.C., and a detachment of the Company led the procession to St. Paul's at a Thanksgiving For Peace.)

1827.   Order in Council disbands those Volunteer Corps which during the preceding ten years had not been called out to aid the civil power.

1852.   Act for the re-organisation of the Militia. Royal Naval Coast Volunteers formed under control of the Coastguard Service.

1856.   Control of R.N.C.V. passed to Admiralty.

1859.   War Office Circular by General Peel sanctions formation of rifle volunteer corps and artillery volunteer corps under the Volunteer Act of 1803. Royal Naval Reserve (Volunteer) Act passed.

1862.   100 leagues service limit for R.N.C.V. abolished and "service anywhere" introduced.

1865.   "National Voluntary Artillery Association" formed.

1871.   Mr. Cardwell introduces Army estimates of £15,000,000 providing for militia, volunteers and yeomanry in addition to regulars, the whole to be unified and controlled by the War Office.

1872.   War Office circular changes title of militia, yeomanry and volunteers from "Reserve Forces" to "Auxiliary Forces", the Pensioners and Army Reservists being styled "Reserve Forces".

1873.   Royal Naval Artillery Volunteers formed. War Office

Circular sanctions formation of Brigade depots of Militia, Yeomanry and Volunteers.

1889. Name of Royal Malta Fencible Artillery changed to Royal Malta Artillery. With this action the word "Fencible" disappeared from the military vocabulary.

1891. Royal Naval Artillery Volunteers disbanded.

1899. South African war starts. Formation of Imperial Yeomanry and raising of Volunteer companies for South Africa.

1900. Scottish Horse (Aberdeen T.A.) formed in South Africa.

1902. National Service League formed.

1903. Mr. Arnold-Forster appointed Secretary for War and introduces proposals for reorganising Army. Royal Naval Volunteer Reserve and Royal Marines Reserve formed.

1904. Norfolk Commission on Auxiliary Forces appointed.

1905. Mr. Arnold-Forster introduces Militia Bill (stillborn by dissolution of Government).

1906. Liberals win election. Richard Burton Haldane becomes War Minister and starts Army reform by appointing General Staff.

1907. Territorial and Reserve Forces Act passed.

1908. March 16th. Special Army Order forming O.T.C. for schools and universities.

April 1st. Statute regarding Territorial Force comes into operation. Old Volunteers and Yeomanry transferred to Territorial Force.

1910. Aeroplane construction starts at Farnborough.

1911. Air Battalion of Royal Engineers formed.

1913. Royal Flying Corps formed.

1914. August 4th. Great War starts. September, first T.F. units go overseas.

1915. Observer Corps formed.

1922. Territorial Force renamed Territorial Army and members undertook to serve overseas if necessary.

1925. Formation of Auxiliary Air Force.

1936. Rapid expansion of anti-aircraft and coastal defence units. Formation of Royal Air Force Volunteer Reserve.

1939. Territorial Army expanded to 212,000 men.

1945. Old Territorial Army stands down.

1947. Territorial Army reconstituted.

1967. Territorial Army Volunteer Reserve formed.

INDEX

INDEX